THE
DREAM
A Journey of Self Discovery

THE DREAM

A Journey of Self Discovery

by Chris Taylor

GOOSE FLATS PUBLISHING, TOMBSTONE - ARIZONA

THE DREAM
A Journey of Self Discovery

by Chris Taylor

©2018 Christopher Taylor

ISBN# 978-1-939345-18-9

Library of Congress Control Number: 2018946299

First Edition June 2018

Book Layout & Design by Keith Davis - Goose Flats Graphics

Cover image of Machu Picchu by Camille Davis at
camilledavisart.com

Published by
Goose Flats Publishing
P.O. Box 813
Tombstone, Arizona, 85638
www.gooseflats.com

Dedicated to:

My Mom who has always supported me in everything I have ever attempted.

My sister Carol without whose help and encouragement this book would not have been written.

And my Dad who was the most honorable man I have ever met.

The Dream

Acknowledgements

A heartfelt thanks to all the doctors and nurses I have had the pleasure to meet. Although we didn't always see eye to eye, they have all been incredible people doing the best that they possibly can in a somewhat broken medical system. I owe my life to them several times over!

Daniel Stone, an amazing teacher and the creator of The Centre of the Conscious Dream in the desert of San Luis Potosi, Mexico. Master dreamer, author and artist. His teachings are practical shamanic tools that will change your life!

Lesley, Simon and Marc Myburgh are spiritual light workers and creators of the magical Mountain House Retreat at the Temple of the Moon just outside Cusco, Peru. Thank you for an awesome San Pedro ceremony in one of the most beautiful places on Earth!

Pulse Tours, the nucleus of which is opening an unbelievable new retreat named the Soltara Healing Center in Paquera, Puntarenas Costa Rica. Thanks for a life-changing Ayahuasca experience! I recommend them highly for a safe ceremony that pays homage to the traditions and spirituality that is so important in working with the Mother Ayahuasca.

The Clinica de Terapias Biologicas and Dr. Jesus Gonzalo Navaro Sota, the holistic empath who specializes in the use of the Mora machine. Thanks for helping me to turn the corner.

Inventor Byington Sims, the owner of Aquatronics in Bisbee, Arizona. The inventor of the galvanic bath, the life saving machine that people are too afraid to use.

And lastly to Steve, cannabis farmer and healer who produced the phoenix tears that helped me through the darkest hours.

Foreword
Connections

My first introduction to Chris was at Porch Jams. We had been attending this Sunday celebration of friends, music and food for a few months and I had been introduced to so many wonderful people who were fast becoming dear friends. Although I had seen Chris a few times, the occasion to visit with him and get to know him never seemed to present itself. His visits were brief, usually spent in conversation with Snake and Raven, but always leaving me wondering who he was.

Perhaps it was what I saw in his eyes that first captivated my attention. There was a transparency of soul within those blue eyes. There was serenity that radiated from his eyes and filled the space he held. I felt there must be a story within their depths; a story that I sensed I needed to know. Or possibly it was his smile that first drew me towards his aura. It, like his eyes, spoke of truth and unencumbered peace. His smile would draw me in, leaving me wondering about the story behind the pure love that radiated from within.

I waited for the opportunity to delve into the man behind the smile and blue eyes, never expecting for it to present itself in the publication of this book. And, thankfully, once I did that deep dive into his journey, once I read his words that took me along on his personal journey of self-discovery, I understood, I knew our meeting was destined and I finally knew exactly what it was that called my attention to this special man. He had called me into his Dream!

But I digress; allow me to go back to how I came to be involved with publishing this book and all the connections. It was a beautiful Porch Jams Sunday and Chris and Chapo were slowly approaching the gathering of friends seated outside. There was something different about him that day. His aura, the glow from his eyes and smile was more than radiant, it appeared ecstatic and I soon learned why. He spoke to Raven and Snake about finishing his book. They appeared so thrilled for his accomplishment and hugs were shared all around. I had no idea there was a book to convey the story behind what I saw in his eyes, but felt that, perhaps, this book he spoke of would be a catalyst to understanding this beautiful soul that radiated in our presence. I listened a bit closer and hoped to hear what I felt destined to. Had he found a publisher yet, Raven asked. No, he replied stating that he just finished it two days ago and was not sure where to go from here. This was it! He had not found a publisher. I called over to him saying, "I know a publisher that can help you." "Seriously," he replied with a look of surprise. "Yes," I responded, my arm pointing back toward me. At that same time, Raven spoke up and seconded that thought while also pointing at me. "Janice is a publisher," she shared with her friend. Chris had no idea that Keith and I owned a publishing business but, upon hearing the news, his smile beamed just a bit more radiantly.

He had not thought that Sunday afternoon that his Dream could possibly bring a publisher into his path, nor did he expect to go home that afternoon and send the email off to me that would open the door to seeing *The Dream* published and fulfill a promise made to speak about the story of his journey of self-discovery, spiritual connections and euphoric experiences.

I had agreed to read his submission, and I was about to learn the secret behind his glow. I was about to become the last connection along this part of his journey.

The Dream, although a journey of healing, both physically and spiritually, is also a story of the connections we make in our individual journeys this lifetime. And that Sunday afternoon where beautiful, like-minded friends met for music, conversation and good food seemed to be the perfect place for Chris to find the connection to complete this part of his story and his Dream.

It wasn't long after Chris first met Snake through mutual friends that the invitation to join him and Raven on Sunday at Porch Jams was offered and the connections began. An introduction to someone who suggested a natural way to respond to his physical nemesis was made one Sunday; resulting in both relief from some pain for him and complete surprise to the physicians treating him! A connection thread was extended towards Steve, who would bring relief by supplying precious drops of "phoenix tears", and with those, came a desire to nourish his body again. Byington always shows up at Porch Jams with stories of healing and, thankfully, Chris consented to welcome him into his Dream as well, much to the condemnation of the medical world. It was a meeting at Porch Jams that opened the way for him to purchase the land he calls home today – a perfect place, suited just right for this Dreamer. And ultimately, the publishing of this book has come through yet another Porch Jams connection!

Chris's narrative will take you on a journey that, for all intents and purposes, is exclusively his but nonetheless, includes many others in his Dream. Facing near death experiences and eventually being reawakened with an immense sense of loving life, he found his way to what can only be called, transcendence.

The calling from the Mother Ayahuasca, the Dream of Machu Picchu and the journey towards understanding his purpose, along with the time spent in the presence of spiritual healers, shamans, and friends met along the way are all part of this extraordinary tale. All part of the story that, should you be reading this now, has also captured you in *The Dream* of Chris Taylor, lover of life and deliverer of a promise.

Perhaps we will never venture our way to Machu Picchu and partake in ancient ceremonial rituals. Perhaps we may never make it to Mexico to study with master dreamers and artists. And perhaps we may never face life-threatening circumstances such that Chris dealt with.

But, perhaps, just perhaps, by reading this book, you too, like I do now, will understand the deep and unending love of life we all could have, if we just Dream it.

With appreciation to Chris for allowing me to be a part of his Dream,

Janice Hendricks ~ Goose Flats Publishing

Prologue
Dios mio! Her eyes!

They were at once youthful and ancient! They brimmed with compassion and were as cold as ice! Bright with inquisitiveness and deep as the ocean! They held the promise of all that is, was and ever will be! How easy it would be to lose oneself in their depths! The truths and knowledge that might be found there! I knew instinctively that in going there I would be forever lost. There would be no return! This was undoubtedly the entity who had spent the last 5 days tormenting me.

It was she! I had been granted audience with the Mother Ayahuasca! She was ancient yet beautiful beyond words or comprehension! Here was a being that transcended time and dimensions and she was smiling at me as if I was her favorite child!

I had traveled thousands of miles and spent countless hours trying to ready myself mentally for this possibility! No amount of written or spoken word could prepare me for this encounter and I knew that my whole life had been leading up to this moment.

My reverie was broken when I realized that she was speaking. I did not hear these words as much as they seemed to materialize as concepts in my head. Her words did not come from any language; it was pure thought. She was inside my head and I would be hiding nothing from her. Her demand was clear to me. She wished to know what had brought me here?!

I formed the answer that she surely already knew...

But wait! It seems I am already well ahead of myself in this story! Perhaps I should explain why I had been summoned from my somewhat ordinary life in Bisbee, Arizona to the headwaters of the Amazon to meet this fantastically resplendent creature in the first place?

The Dream

Chapter One
Falling to Pieces

My journey began with a small piece of calcium. I had experienced these floating pebbles moving around in my body before and knew that these sharp little deposits can be brutally painful.

This particular little stone, however; was bent on proving to be unusually malicious. That it had formed in my pancreas was not unheard of, but it had lodged itself into and partially blocked the duct through which my digestive enzymes flowed. This was not a common occurrence and not an easy diagnosis. Unable to exit my pancreas, the enzymes then began digesting the only thing available to them - my pancreas itself. The result of this blockage was excruciating pancreatic attacks that were akin to being run thru with a sword of fire!

Unfortunately for me, my doctors were unable to locate this stone and the cause of my monthly attacks and accompanying stays in the hospital went undiagnosed.

What followed was two years of hell in the form of monthly chronic attacks of pancreatitis. These attacks took an accumulative effect on my body to the point where I could keep nothing down and my body began to shut down. Still unaware of the stone that was causing me all this grief, the doctors said that the only thing they could offer me was the removal of a cyst that had developed in my pancreas. This involved the surgical removal of half of my pancreas and my spleen. As I saw it I had no choice. If I did nothing I would die. I relented to a surgery I was unsure of. As I entered the hospital I had little hope that it would be successful and less that I would survive.

I awoke bristling with tubes. While my medical condition was no better, (the stone was still lodged in my duct blocking my pancreas), something miraculous did happen on that operating table. I woke up with a fierce desire to live and an immense gratefulness for another chance! Something had changed in my psychological makeup. Gone were any desires for wealth and success. My priorities had been upended! Those things that used to drive me had been replaced by the wish to live life to the fullest! Small things like smiles and kindnesses were more important now. I would now live in each moment and things like nature and friendships shown in a new light! I felt as though I was coming out of a lifelong slumber! To paraphrase a line from a Buffalo Springfield song, "I've got reason to live! I've got things I can give!"

I would need every bit of my newfound love of life as my nemesis, the stone, was not yet through with me.

My pancreatic attacks and regular hospital visits resumed. The doctors were at a loss and after another painful stint in the hospital one of their scans finally paid off. My little rock had made its presence known! Finally, the reason for all my tribulations was exposed. We now knew the cause of my chronic pancreatitis. The little piece of calcium was strangling my pancreas. The tricky part was how to remove it?

Since pancreatic stones are rare, other accepted methods of breaking up renal stones such as lithotripsy are not approved methods of treatment by the FDA. The only method that the doctors could come up with to remove the stone was a procedure called an ERCP. This entailed going down through my throat with a scope to access my pancreas through my stomach and trying to grab the stone and pull it out.

Unfortunately, my antagonist proved to be too big to pull out through my bile duct. The doctor left a piece of plastic called a stent in the bile duct to stretch it out in hopes that they could go back in again and pull it through. During the next year the doctors would make four more unsuccessful attempts to pull the stone out; each time leaving more stents to stretch the bile duct.

The doctors were frustrated and my repeated pancreatic attacks and incursions by the doctors into my pancreas via ERCP were taking their toll on me. I was informed that the doctors would make one final attempt at removing the stone. If unsuccessful, they wanted to perform another major operation in which they would remove the remaining portion of my pancreas and rearrange my existing organs to make things work. I would be a type 1 diabetic with untold future complications!

I have the utmost respect and gratitude for my doctors and their efforts. Everyone has their own views on the state of medical care in the United States and I believe that without their care I would have passed away, but it is my opinion that certain illnesses are better treated holistically.

I began looking for alternative methods for dealing with stones. In my quest for answers I met someone that would change my whole view of medicine.

He simply asked me why I was subjecting myself to all this torture at the hands of the doctors. Why didn't I just take matters into my own hands and get rid of the stone myself? I had no idea that I was capable of this or I would have done it a year ago. I told him I had a month before my next and last ERCP and I would try anything to make my stone go away! He told me that if I did what he said my stone would be gone.

I was to do a cleanse that consisted of solely lemon water and apple cider with Cayenne pepper. I could have a bowl of oatmeal once a week and I was to take certain supplements.

I asked him how long. He asked me how bad I wanted to get rid of the stone. I told him that I was determined not to let them cut me again and if I couldn't get rid of this stone, I might die. He said to keep up the cleanse as long as I possibly could.

I lasted three weeks. By the end I was again skinny as a rail, looking like a POW and making children cry. I was starting to have visions and dizzy spells. I really needed to eat! I had one week to get some strength back before my final ERCP.

I went in for my procedure feeling like I had no control of my life and my life and future was being determined by a small piece of calcium. While I had found a new love for this life, I was not sure I would get to enjoy it. My life for the last three years had been a sort of hell and it seemed as though my future hinged on this procedure. As I checked myself in I couldn't help but feel the presence of a reaper lurking behind me, biding its time!

I emerged from my procedure with the familiar feeling of my head being stuffed with cotton. As usual, I began taking stock of my body and my surroundings. As was his want, my doctor came to my bed before I had a chance to clear my head and began talking animatedly. He was excited and all I really got out of his soliloquy was the fact that the stone crumbled before his eyes as he went to grab it and he had never seen anything like it before!

At last I was free of my nemesis!

After four years of agony I had a new lease on life!

Thru all my trials in the last four years I had come to realize a few truths. One being that my perception of life had taken an abrupt about face! It was as if I was once again a child and seeing the world for the first time! I saw beauty in small things that I never noticed before. My anger and frustrations with people in my life was replaced by gratitude and empathy. I was indeed living each moment as if it was my first or my last. I no longer cared about success or money or material things. My goal now was to live every moment as though it was my last and to seek out the wonders and mysteries that I had spent my whole life ignoring.

During my dealings with the multitude of doctors that had come along with my affliction I had lost confidence in the medical system as practiced in the United States. While I had respect for the doctors themselves, I had come to totally disagree with some of their practices such as treating the symptoms and not trying for a cure. I had no doubt that it was the cleanse that had dissolved the stone. I had come to the awareness that we are not victims in our illnesses, and that we have the power to prevent them by living in harmony with our bodies and environment. I had spent the first part of my life living as though I was invincible and now I knew, that if I didn't treat my body as a temple, then my future was going to be bleak.

I now had a half of a pancreas and no spleen. My ability to digest food and my immune system were forever compromised. I realized now that my life would never be the same, and if I was to have some semblance of a normal life, I needed to come to terms with my condition and make drastic changes in my lifestyle in order to survive.

But I had a second chance! I was determined not to waste it! I vowed to spend what time I had left in seeking out some of the truths and mysteries of life that we so studiously ignore until we get that big wakeup call.

Armed with my newfound love of life, the realization that I had blundered through the first fifty years of my life with blinders on, feeling relatively healthy for the first time in memory, and free of my shackles, I set out on the biggest journey of my life. It was to be a journey of self-discovery. A metamorphosis of mind and body that would take me to strange, dangerous and beautiful places that I had only dreamt about. I had emerged from my cocoon and was itching to try out my new wings! I had no idea how, but I was determined to make the most out of every moment that had been granted!

In my journey I would meet teachers and healers. I would study with shamans and confront my demons. I would see and experience things that I could never have imagined. These teachings and travels would forge me into a different creature and give me the skills and tools to fight the biggest battle of my life!

Chapter Two
Summoned

I drifted lazily toward the dawning light of consciousness. I was in no hurry. I was trying to remember the details of my dream. The hard edges of my dream softened and grew fuzzy as I opened my eyes to the morning. From the texture of the light and the coolness of the air I could tell it was going to be a cold rainy day in Bisbee. Yes, we have those days in Arizona too.

Being reluctant to leave the warmth of my bed, I decided to put off my normal waking routine and consider my dream. It was relatively easy because I had dreamt the same dream several times in the last week. I had never been pestered by a dream before like this.

In my dream I was in a dark, smoky room filled with an otherworldly singing. It seemed to be a ceremony of some kind, but my Catholic upbringing offered no comparisons. I could sense others in the room, but they were shrouded in darkness. Through the gloom and tobacco filled haze there was a shadowy figure cavorting in front of me. He seemed to be the source of the song and was caught up in a ritualized ceremony of some kind. He stopped his singing and stood before me. I could just make him out and the air seemed to weigh heavily on my skin. Something was not right. I felt as if I was underwater and everything was in slow motion. The shadow figure before me took a draught off a bottle and spit some foul-smelling liquid at me! It was the shock of this action that shook me free of my dream's clutches.

The dream was not frightening, but it nagged at me. I took a quick look at the drizzle outside and made a bowl of oatmeal and crawled back into bed. I had nothing pressing to do and it was looking like a day for a good book. I clicked on the television to see if anything of importance transpired while I slept, but bored quickly and I turned it to a documentary to watch while I ate breakfast. The subject of the film was Machu Picchu in Peru. I could watch and learn about Machu Picchu endlessly as it is a place that exudes magic and had been a fascination of mine for as long as I could remember.

I quickly learned the film was not just about Machu Picchu, but about Peru itself, and it looked at the people and their culture also. I knew that up until the 1500's Peru was the most powerful country in South America. Although Peru was the center of the Incan empire, its boundaries reached as far as Chile in the south and Ecuador in the north. They built an amazing road system throughout their immense kingdom and were master masons. They were very spiritual people and their main deity was Pachamama or Mother Earth. In the early part of the 15th century Peru was besieged by a plague in the form of Spanish conquistadors. These inhuman parasites were driven by greed, and although they traveled under the guise of ambassadors for Catholicism, their main deity was gold. In the name of their religion they utterly destroyed the amazing Incan civilization. The Spanish were not content to rob the country of its riches; they were intent on wiping the once proud Incas from the face of the earth. In 1532 the last Inca king was drawn and quartered in the main square of Cusco, the Incan capital. What followed was centuries of destruction of everything Incan. Temples were torn down and replaced with cathedrals where the people were forced to worship a foreign god.

I was thoroughly engrossed by the documentary when I started to get an uneasy feeling. The film was talking about religion and the fact that the Peruvian people were beginning to shrug off the influence of the Catholicism that had been forced on them, and they were reverting to the beliefs of their ancestors, the Incans. The hairs on the back of my neck started rising as the film delved into an ancient medicine that was an integral part of their indigenous religion. The medicine was called Ayahuasca, and it was a powerful hallucinogenic concoction that, when administered by a shaman, was purported to have amazing curative properties. They used it to treat any number of maladies from emotional trauma to cognitive disorders and even cancer! The reel went on to observe a traditional Ayahuasca ceremony and I was astonished when I realized that I was witnessing an exact replica of my disturbing dream!

The fact that my troubling dream had depicted this same ancient indigenous ceremony floored me! I am not one to believe in coincidences and what I saw that rainy morning left me deeply disturbed. I spent the next two days researching everything I could find about Ayahuasca, Peru, and Machu Picchu.

Several months had passed since I had passed the stone and my strength had grown daily. I had won a three-year long battle with the government and was now drawing a disability paycheck. The delay was a blessing in retrospect as I had been due two years back pay. As can be imagined I had accrued substantial debts, but I had a little leftover after settling my debts.

While I was feeling better than I had in years, I knew in my heart that my health issues were not over. They had removed half my pancreas and my spleen and my immune system and digestion were going to be an issue for me the remainder of my life. I realized that to stay healthy I was going to need to adhere to a strict diet, and in order to avoid catching every bug floating around, I would need to keep my body in shape. I needed to get in touch with my body in a way that I had been evading my whole life. Up until my operation I had thought myself invincible. I had given little regard to my body and was pretty sure that my health problems had been a direct result. I wanted to relearn how to eat! I yearned for a simple, pure life. I wanted to walk the walk! This was not a lifestyle choice as much as a necessity if I was going to keep going on in this incarnation.

My newfound love for life had not diminished, but was instead blossoming! I knew now that I had wasted my life to this point trying to live up to the American ideal. The problem was now that none of that mattered to me anymore. I had no idea how much time I had left, and I was determined not to waste any of it! It was as if I was becoming aware that there is so much more happening all around us that we are oblivious to.

My parents had fostered an open-minded childhood. I can remember reading "Chariots of the Gods" when I was ten. I believed our government had done an admirable job of keeping its wards ignorant and in fear. I longed to shed the bonds of its systematic suppression of individuality and freedom of thought. There was a huge, wondrous world full of mysteries at every turn which I had spent my life studiously ignoring! And above all, I wanted to find out the reason for my existence. Why did I have this desire to live? I had wasted my youth chasing success and the American way and now I had been given another chance. I had a nagging feeling that I was still here for a reason. That I had yet to fulfill my destiny!

Now was the time to start my journey! There was a whole world full of answers out there and I was armed with an infinite arsenal of questions! I felt with certainty that I knew now where I needed to begin.

~•~

I began making preparations for a foray to Peru. I was convinced it was my destiny to follow my dream and that I had been called there. If I could but replicate my dream, I felt that some essential knowledge would be revealed to me that I would be in need of if I was to continue on my odyssey. Possibly I might find insights into how to live my life in harmony and thrive with the restrictions that had been forced on me.

In my investigations I had come across a tour group that not only went to Machu Picchu but also offered Ayahuasca ceremonies with a shaman in the Amazon. I felt that to journey into that place by myself would be foolhardy in the least, and a group of like-minded people seemed the prudent course.

I booked my reservations for June and I began preparing for what would turn out to be a journey of a lifetime. Joining this group was no coincidence for me, but a matter of destiny. This was to be no vacation, but a spiritual awakening that would set my lifelong ideals on end.

Chapter Three
Father San Pedro

We shrugged free of the perpetual fog that seemed to envelope Lima and it was immediately apparent that we were bound to dash ourselves on the immense slab of rock that loomed ahead! After the shock, it was also apparent that my sentiment was premature. I had underestimated our pilot's skill and he seemed up to the task of summiting the majestic Andes that towered over the horizon. I had managed to wrangle a window seat and it was about to pay off!

I had flown over the Rockies and Sierra Nevadas but they were little sisters compared to this palisade! I was blessed with clear skies, and for the next hour and a half I sat mesmerized by the peaks and glaciers of the longest mountain range in the world. It is only bested in height by the behemoths in Asia. I tried my best and could swear that I saw the legendary Incan highways snaking through the passes. A good portion of the range was above tree line and the terrain looked frigid and inhospitable in its stark beauty.

I was prodded from my reverie by the sound of the pilot's voice announcing our decent to Cusco. I remember thinking this was surely a bit early as we were still high up in the rocky slopes. As we dropped from the icy peaks the terrain softened a bit and green swathes of flora could be seen making inroads into the rocky landscape. The plane made a sharp bank and there was Cusco nestled like a jewel in the crook of the mountainside.

One can only imagine what Cusco must have been like prior to the Spanish invasion. The city was said to be laid out in the form of a puma with a river running through the center. Garcilaso de la Vega, one of the Spanish conquistadors, chronicled that the temple to the Sun God featured a large disc of solid gold and inlaid with precious stones that represented their mightiest deity. The sacred garden in front of the temple had "plants with leaves of beaten gold, stems of silver, solid gold corn-cobs and twenty life-size llamas and their herders made of pure gold."

The Incas were superior masons to their conquerors, but the Spanish were so intent on wiping out all evidence of their victims that the foundations are all there is remaining of the fabulous Incan temples. Since no drawings of Cusco survived the purge, all we have to go on are the written accounts given by Spanish scribes and their eyes were only for gold. Suffice it to say that one of the most beautiful cities ever to grace the earth was erased from our memory.

Modern day Cusco, though bearing little resemblance to its ancestor, is also an amazing and beautiful city.

The colonial architecture with terraces overlooking the narrow cobblestone streets gives it a European flavor. The millions of people who come here from every corner of the world on their way to neighboring Machu Picchu give it an international feel. The locals are colorful people inside and out. They are hardworking, friendly, happy and very spiritual. The city is alive with music, restaurants and seemingly endless festivals. It took very little time for Cusco and its people to put me under their spell.

I had arrived two days prior to my scheduled meet with the tour group and I wished I had allowed more time. My taxi ride from the airport turned comical when the driver could not find my hostel among the narrow cobblestone streets. Very little of Cusco is on flat ground and we drove up, down and around asking directions until we got lucky enough to find someone who could guide us. Finally, we stopped in front of an unremarkable stucco façade with a small sign over the single wooden door saying Casa de la Gringa.

I was unprepared for the light and colorful interior of the quaint hostel. I stowed my bags and didn't linger as I was eager to explore. I spent my first afternoon wandering around and soaking in the unique vibe that is Cusco. I visited the huge gold-filled cathedrals on the main square and the endless tourist stores. I walked the busy city center and explored the hilly residential alleys. I marveled at the architecture and its inhabitants. I found them to be open and jovial people; so unlike most of the urban dwellers that I am familiar with. The weather was perfect and the air at 11,000 feet was crisp and fresh.

The steps leading up to one of the ancient cathedrals that dominated the main square seemed a good place to sit in the sun and people watch. The square was packed with people from everywhere, seemingly all speaking different languages. Apparently, there was some rule that a festival of some sorts was always to be happening in the square.

Soon a smiling young man plopped down beside me and said, "Hello sir, how are you today?"

A little taken aback, I replied, "Muy bien. Es un hermoso dia. Y tu?"

"I am well. Con permiso? Can I sit with you? I need to practice my English," he asked.

And so, we went on - he in his surprisingly good English and me in my mediocre Spanish. If we got stuck, we would revert to our own language and we managed to get along just fine. His name was Raul and he was a student at the famous art school in town. He was full of questions and answers and he made me laugh. After a while, he produced a satchel with some strikingly colorful watercolors of Cusco city scenes. He gave me what I thought was a great deal on one of them and I didn't have to haggle, which is not my favorite thing to do. I had mentioned that I would like to visit the ruins of Saksaywaman the next day and he offered to be my guide. This sounded more appealing than a tour group and we agreed to meet the next morning.

There were enticing aromas from the vast number of restaurants catering to the myriads of tourists, but I suddenly realized the flight and the elevation had taken their toll on me. I stumbled back up the hill and it only took me about a half hour before I found my hostel by pure luck. My coma-like sleep was shattered by fireworks at dawn as there was a celebration of some sort going on down the street. I would find that Cusco didn't have time for such things as sleep.

Raul was waiting in the square with his perpetual smile and we took a short taxi ride to Saksaywaman which was just outside the city limits. Raul talked seemingly without ever pausing for breath and he turned out to be an excellent and enthusiastic guide. As we drove, he pointed out groups of people gathered in the fields and he explained that they were doing rituals honoring Pachamama, the earth mother of their indigenous religion. He went on to say that the people of Peru, while not completely free of the influence of the religion that had been forced on them by the Conquistadors, were reverting to their original beliefs. The primary deities being the Sun God and the Earth mother. The people were very spiritual and in touch with the land.

Ever since I was I kid I have been drawn to ancient Indian sites. Arizona is the home of thousands of these sites and as a kid I would often come across evidence of our ancestors. I was always intrigued and felt an amazing connection to these places. In time, I developed a gift of being able to look out over the desert landscape and be able to pick out the places where the ancient people might have stayed for a time. If I have a chance to sit quietly and look and listen I can often feel the presence of the ancients. I have such respect and reverence for these sites that they have become like places of magic to me.

A few special times I have even sworn I could see visages and ghosts of the elders going about their business.

Although I had visited many ancient sites, I was unprepared for what I saw at the citadel of Saksaywaman. It is one of those mysteries that the archeological community does not like to talk about. The fortress was supposedly built by the Kilke culture around 1,000 AD. The walls of the complex are of huge stones that are fitted together like jigsaw puzzles with seamless joints and no mortar. No one knows where these huge boulders came from or how they were assembled. The technology is well beyond what can be accomplished with the tools available at the time. Indeed, we would have no idea how to go about it with modern day tools. Raul said that the people believed that the ancients had "melted" the stones and then cut them with knives. The Inca culture then added on to the existing fortress in the 13th century.

The real mystery is that while the Incas were master masons, they didn't hold a candle to the work of the Kilke culture. The portion of the walls added on by the Incas looks almost childish in comparison to the work of the people just two hundred years before them. How was all that knowledge lost in that short of time span? Indeed, how can we not be able to duplicate it today?

This is one of the mysteries that make Cusco and Peru an enchanting place that brings out the inner child in me. I believe that there are a lot of things in our world that are unexplained or just kept from the general public. The archeological community chooses to ignore these contradictions to their established beliefs, but the evidence is mounting to the point where they are going to have to restructure the whole timeline of human history. Better yet, they could admit that they have no idea. This was an incredible beginning to my journey of self-discovery in this place of enlightenment.

As we went back to the city, I was amazed by the colorful garb of the locals. To me it is a reflection of their outlook on life. Outside the city it was obvious that they did not have much abundance here. Yet from their appearance one had to believe that they are a happy and prosperous people. It dawned on me that these people were content in their way of life even though it was not full of all the things that people in the States take for granted. This, and their affinity for hard work and festivities, seemed to me to be a very noble way of life. I found that I respected these spiritually awakened people and that they had a lot to teach the rest of the world in the way of respecting the planet. Not that the rest of mankind would take the time to listen.

I thanked Raul for his generosity and headed back to the hostel. It only took me two wrong turns to get my bearings this time. I got back in time to start meeting some of the other members of the tour group. I had been a little leery about what my traveling companions would be like. I mostly travel in small groups of friends or family. I was pleasantly surprised by the interesting array of personalities who were to make up our group! They seemed to be mostly young people from all over the world. I was to be the elder of the group, but that didn't seem to be a problem, and everyone seemed to be amiable and interesting. My fear of being stuck with a bunch of unbearable strangers was proving to be unfounded. I couldn't believe my good fortune! Tomorrow we would be going to The Temple of the Moon to do a San Pedro ceremony!

~•~

One of the many street dogs that roamed Cusco's cobblestone streets took it upon himself to wake me even before the sun rose, so I was up drinking tea as our group slowly began gathering in the hostel's courtyard. Half the group had already been to the retreat on the Amazon and done the Ayahuasca portion of their tour; Cusco and Machu Picchu being the second half of their trip. They seemed to be as close as family and they each had a unique kind of glow about them! I was truly impressed by these young adults from around the globe who had traveled vast distances on their own to gather here in a foreign country to seek knowledge and to better themselves. They were some of the nicest young people I have ever met, and it was to be my honor to travel with them for the next week. Four others, like me, were on the first half of their trip and we would all be going to the Amazon later for the second portion of our journey.

I was a bit surprised and intrigued when a beautiful young woman introduced herself as Tatyana and started organizing the group. Tatyana appeared a little young to be leading a tour group in a third world country. She was blond and fair-skinned and had perfect features that gave her an elfin quality. She also had an unflappable, rather ethereal demeanor which would serve her well while guiding a group in a country where very little seemed to go as planned. Tatyana would prove to be a very powerful and compassionate spiritual guide as well. I was beginning to feel very fortunate in my choice of tour groups.

The streets of Cusco are very narrow and traffic was blocked while our group hurriedly tried to get ourselves and our luggage stored into two vans. Finally, much to the relief of the cars piling up in the street behind us, the two over-stuffed vans were ready for the trip to the Mountain House Retreat. Luckily the trip was a short one as the retreat was only a few kilometers outside of Cusco.

The Mountain House Retreat is a beautiful compound located adjacent to the ancient Temple of the Moon in the Sacred Valley of the Incas. The retreat consists of a large main house, a smaller house and various huts that surround an incredible garden filled with unfamiliar plants of every hue imaginable! The place exuded a serenity and tranquility that made one want to whisper.

The Mountain House is run by Lesley Myburgh and her two sons Simon and Mark. Lesley is a renowned medicine woman originally from South Africa who has been living in Cusco and working with the San Pedro/Wachuma medicine since the late nineties. Lesley wouldn't be present at our ceremony, but the space she has manifested in this holy valley is truly amazing! Her sons Simon and Mark would be the spiritual guides on our journey, and the ceremony would be presided over by Shaman Luis Quispe of the Queros people. As were most of his people, Don Luis was short in stature, but I cannot remember ever being in the presence of anyone who radiated such goodwill! He had a perpetual smile that was almost impossible not to respond to. He would be my cheerful spiritual guide in the ceremony to come.

We stowed our bags where directed, as we would be staying the night, and started gathering in the thatched circular ceremonial hut that was called a Maloca. Our group was joined by a few others who had other arrangements so there were around twenty of us that were eventually seated in a circle on the wooden floor. This was as diverse a group as one could imagine. We were from all walks of life, young and old, and each of us had journeyed here for different reasons.

Simon started by stating that San Pedro is a sacred cactus used in the Andes for thousands of years to heal on emotional, spiritual and physical levels. Locally known as Wachuma, the medicine helps us to grow, learn, and awaken, and it helps us to reach higher states of consciousness. It can help us to connect with the most revered Mother Earth or Pachamama. It can help give a greater understanding of our purpose in life and love for ourselves and all of creation. He referred to this sacred plant medicine as "the Father" or "the Light." When we got to the jungles of the Amazon later in our trip we would work with Ayahuasca. She is referred to as "the Mother" or "the Darkness." He explained that after drinking the medicine we would most likely purge ourselves of the drink. In other words, we would throw it back up! Not to worry though, as this was perfectly normal and wouldn't diminish the powerful effect of the medicine, and that our discomfort would not last long. There were small buckets placed around the grounds for this purpose. To me, the purging was like an act of faith on our part. We were willing to submit to this small humility in order for the Father medicine to bestow his blessings on us.

Simon spoke in English as everyone here, with the exception of Shaman Luis, spoke it as a first or second language. He asked us to introduce ourselves and share our intentions for the ceremony if we would. Every single one of us had come for a different reason. We went around the circle stating our intent. The reasons varied from seeking healing of an emotional or physical nature, to just trying to expand their consciousness in an incredible setting. I was unduly nervous and not all that sure that I wanted to share my reasons with everyone, but the others were so honest and forthcoming that I knew no one here would pass any judgments on me.

I told them briefly of my many trials and tribulations regarding my health and expressed that I knew that I had a rough road ahead of me and that I was trying to find a new way of living that would allow me to recover from my operation and live a clean "normal" life. I had stopped drinking when they told me I had chronic pancreatitis and I was willing, at this point, to make whatever changes in my lifestyle that would allow me to thrive. I was hoping to be shown a path to follow on this journey that is my life. I was looking for some kind of balance between my spiritual and physical self that would let me overcome my new physical limitations.

Telling my story would prove to be the hardest part of what was to be an amazing day. Everyone I spoke to wished me encouragement on my quest and I returned their sentiment just as sincerely. Simon started pouring a green slimy looking concoction into cups and passed them around the circle. We all said a brief prayer to the Father and drank down the medicine. It proved to be just as slimy as it appeared but not as bad as I feared. Simon told us to go out and enjoy the garden, to lie down on the mats scattered about if we felt queasy and after we purged we would feel much better.

It was a large garden with many wonders and each of us meandered into it seeking a space where we could lie down peacefully and pass this first and most difficult part of the ceremony. I was not ready to lie down, so I aimlessly explored the garden. I became more and more enchanted with the amazing array of plants, some of which I had never seen before. The day was a perfect temperature, somewhere in the 70's, with the tiniest of breezes to keep the air moving. This was the most beautiful place I had ever been! It was as if I had never been in a garden before. Surely these were the most amazing flowers in the world! I was beginning to feel a oneness with my surroundings. I became aware of insects and lizards and an abundance of life that I had not noticed before.

I was suddenly aware that Simon and Shaman Luis were standing nearby regarding me with bemused expressions. Simon approached and he asked, "How are you feeling Chris? Have you purged yet?"

"I am wonderful," I replied. And I was!

"Why don't you come lay down on a mat and I will bring you a little more of the sacred plant. Do you think you might like a little more?"

I sat on a nearby mat and looked around at my companions. Most were lying quietly, but I could hear a few of them ridding themselves of the medicine. Shaman Luis was going from one to the other and doing ritual blessings. His blessing varied, but usually involved chanting and rattles! Simon returned with another cup of the plant medicine and just as quickly left me in peace. This time it wasn't long before I was reaching for a bucket and before I knew it I had rejected the slimy cactus brew! And that was the extent of my distress.

I was lying on my back watching the clouds change from one image to the next like an animated film when Shaman Luis appeared above me and began giving me his blessing for a successful ceremony. He danced and sang and sprinkled some kind of aromatic liquid on my head. His rhythmic beat and song were hypnotic, and I was transported. I seemed to witness his dance from someplace above. Then he was done, and I felt extremely blessed to be alive! I was very aware of my breath and the purity of the mountain air! The colors were more vivid! The smells and sounds more crisp and clear!

A woman who introduced herself as Lesley's sister, Simon's aunt, came and sat at my mat with me. She told me that her husband had passed away from pancreatitis and it was a miracle that I was still here and had the privilege of coming to this place of beauty. She told me that I was blessed and had been given a second chance and that she could tell that I was going to make the most of it! My love of life and my gratitude were shining through she told me, and it was a beautiful thing to watch. I thanked her and knew that her words were true! It was a miracle! And life was a miracle! I had never felt as humbled by the fact that I had been given this opportunity to have this experience we call life!

I now wanted to get up and start exploring this intriguing compound again! Before I could begin my investigations one of the pretty Peruvian women who was employed here brought me the most amazing fruit salad I had ever eaten! There were mangoes, papayas, bananas and pineapple among other things. Each bite was an explosion of flavor! It was like I had never tasted fruit before! All memories of the purging vanished and I felt refreshed and energized.

Simon sauntered by and said he would be leading a group on a hike to the ancient site of Salumpunku, or The Temple of the Moon, and would I like to come along?

Yes! I was going to get to walk through the ancient Sacred Valley and see the carved stone shrines called Huacas that have been here for time immemorial. I eagerly accepted his invitation and gathered with the other adventurers. Everyone seemed vibrant and happy and no worse for having the purging experience. Indeed, it seemed that the people, the plants and even the air were sparkling and all my senses seemed to be heightened.

Simon appeared and led us out the gate and it was just a short walk to the temple and surrounding ruins. The members of our group, being in a state of altered consciousness, were easily distracted by the smallest of things as everything was a wonder. It was like seeing things with a whole different perspective that was more in tune with Mother Nature. I thought Simon did an admirable job of keeping us together and moving along while imparting local wisdom. I doubt if the people of very many countries would welcome a group of people who were obviously impaired into one of their most sacred sites. The locals we met treated us with respect as we were honoring one of their most holy ceremonies and we were honoring their heritage. I found them to be extremely enlightened and accepting of these foreigners trying to learn more of their culture. Shaman Luis would seemingly appear out of the thin air from time to time, always with a huge smile. He was obviously very reverent of this place and he passed this sentiment on to us. From time to time he would conduct small ceremonies directed to Pachamama, the Earth Mother, or possibly the Sun, Condor or Puma gods.

Our hike took us through numerous ruins of temples, many of which were hewn from living rock! Again, it was obvious from the weathering that these ruins were many thousands of years old and made in a time well before the Incan Empire. This is also a touchy subject in the archeological community as they don't believe this area was even inhabited at the time these were made. At one point, Simon pointed out a drawing of what looked like a woolly mammoth although these same scientists believe these went extinct in the Americas over 10,000 years ago. Doesn't add up, but it would be too humiliating to admit that they know very little about the history of this area.

I can't explain the feeling of the power emitted of these ancient sites such as the Temple of the Moon and Salumpunku. Walking through the Sacred Valley was like walking through a vast open-air cathedral. This had been hallowed ground since time immemorial. I have been to Sedona and Mount Shasta and other places the people call power vortexes, but I submit that they don't hold a candle to the pure energy of the Andes and these ancient sites!

We walked through a series of Huacas and sat on thrones carved out of the mountain from which ancient kings had ruled a much different world. Once I managed to sit quietly by myself, and before long, I was seeing visions of ceremonies full of color and pageantry. In these visions the people seemed to be very advanced, almost living an imperial life much like one would expect from the Pharaohs of Egypt.

I walked up to Simon at one point and he was staring at a circular indentation in the rocky landscape. It seemed to be very uniform and I asked him what he thought they had used this for?

"They would hardly have used this for anything," he replied. "I was here yesterday, and this was not here." The ground here was very rocky and would prove to be very hard digging and there was no evidence of manual labor. I asked him what he thought caused it.

"There are a lot of strange things that happen here. Almost every night you can see strange lights in the valley. There are many different opinions about what goes on up here at night and they all involve the supernatural," he explained. Made sense to me. This place seemed like it would be a beacon for UFOs. Lake Titicaca is a famous location for ET sightings and many believe there is an underwater base as strange lights are constantly going into and out of the water.

The highlight of the tour was the Temple of the Moon. It consisted of two stunning caves. In one there was an elaborate alter carved from the rock wall where moonlight would shine on it on certain special nights. I imagined the mystical ceremonies that had been performed here throughout the centuries. There were ancient carvings of snakes and pumas and this shrine had the feeling of being here since creation.

The other cave would house something that would leave me shaken and mystified to this day! The entrance to the cave was natural and uncarved, but it very much resembled a vagina to me. There was a guard outside the cave and Simon explained he was here to enforce a rule that no one was to stay in the cave for more than 15 minutes. Apparently, it was hard to get some people to leave.

As I entered, I was instantly aware that the walls of this cave were burnished to a sheen from thousands of years of human contact. The walls were as smooth as polished marble. The cave wasn't deep and wouldn't hold very many people at once. Again, it is beyond me to describe the feeling permeating this cave. The closest I can come is; it was like re-entering the womb. I felt as if I was in the womb of Mother Earth! And this wasn't the most amazing wonder in this cave! On the floor of the cave was a rock covering a hole. If you moved the rock and put your ear to the hole you could hear and feel what appeared to be the earth breathing. There was a regular intake and exhale of warm air that left you feeling that the cave was an ancient living creature. After hearing the breath of the mountain, I sat back, my mind reeling, but feeling strangely secure in this mountain womb. I had to be reminded that my time was up, and it was time to come back out into the world!

Long before I was ready, Simon told us it was time to go back to the Mountain House as the sun was setting. I was reluctant to leave; this place had a firm hold on me. To me this walk back through time had been more of a religious experience than any in my Catholic upbringing. I sat on the hillside and watched my comrades making their way back to the compound, not wanting to follow. A light touch on my shoulder roused me and rather magically, the effervescent Shaman Luis was there with me.

"Vaminos nino. Tenemos que ir." "Come child, we must go," he urged me gently. I walked back with him pausing every few minutes to examine a rock or piece of pottery that I thought was unbelievably beautiful. He indulged my whims patiently, eyes full of mirth. To this day, I don't believe I have ever met anyone who radiated such a sense of love and harmony. I often think of Shaman Luis when I want to calm myself. He made a huge impression on me and I realized that if I could ever find a balance with myself and nature the way that this man lived his life, it would be the greatest accomplishment I could imagine.

By the time we joined the others some very nice people were dishing out bowls of mouth-watering stew. Like everything else today, it was the best tasting stew I had ever eaten!

Afterwards some of us went out and sat around the campfire and, one by one, started picking up instruments that were conveniently lying around. There was a lot of storytelling as we were all curious about each other. Some of the participants were excellent musicians and singers and some of us just contributed with the beat of a rattle or drum. We talked and sang and played well into the night and I have never felt more at ease with friends or strangers. The effects of the San Pedro broke through all barriers of culture and language; we felt no inhibitions and were able to share our inner-feelings and emotions.

Although the evening was breathtaking, I rather suddenly found I could no longer keep my eyes open. The marvels of the day, while exhilarating, had taken their toll on me. I excused myself from my new-found soul mates and tried to remember where I had left my belongings. After another short tour of the premises, I found what looked like my gear in a dorm room and barely had time to lie down before falling asleep.

I can truly say that this had been one of the most spiritually enlightening days of my life. In the surreal setting of the beautiful retreat and the Sacred Valley with these intelligent and vibrant young strangers I had never felt so close to God and nature. Being a recovering Catholic I wasn't sure I knew who God was. The religions I had researched did not answer my questions. I believed that there was a higher power out there, but I was not sure what form it took. Perhaps I would find my religion here with these spiritual people who seemed so in touch with themselves and nature.

This was no ordinary tour group! This day was to be the beginning of what would be a rather fantastical adventure! In my time in Peru I would learn many things about myself and find a new kind of spirituality. Having come from a place that was void of the spiritual, it was like coming out of a tunnel into the light. I was beginning to see the world with new eyes!

Tomorrow my new friends and I would take the train from Cusco to the small town of Aguas Calientes. The millions of people that visited the town each year do not come for the hot springs. Aguas Calientes was the gateway to one of the wonders of the world and a place that had been calling to me since childhood. In the morning we would set out for Machu Picchu!

Chapter Four
Machu Picchu

I t was dark and raining when Tatyana roused us. We made a rather hurried departure from the beautiful Mountain House. The serene tranquility of the unique retreat would leave a lasting impression on me! This was a place of light and love and I was reluctant to leave! I found solace in the fact that we were leaving this magical place and going to a place that lived in my dreams! The mythical Machu Picchu!

Once again, we stowed our gear and crammed into the two vans for the trip to the train station where we would depart for Aguas Calientes. Tatyana's experience and foresight paid off as one of the vans lost traction and slid off the dirt road on our way back to Cusco. We spent a good bit of time getting wet and muddy, but we were ultimately successful in pushing the van out of the quicksand-filled ditch. We would make it to the train station looking like we had lost a fight but just in time to board.

I was pleasantly surprised by the opulence of the train! It was clean and comfortable and featured gourmet meals and fashion shows! This was no high-speed train as the

90-kilometer trip took a couple of hours. I had no idea that Cusco, at 11,000 feet was over 3,000 feet higher than Machu Picchu. My eyes were glued to the windows as the train made a leisurely descent through the amazing Sacred Valley of the Incas. The valley is in what is called a tropical mountain rain forest, a cloud jungle, and it boasts a lush variety of plants and vines that were unfamiliar to me. Through the dense vegetation I could catch glimpses of ancient stone cities and fortresses that were fighting a losing battle to the ever-encroaching forest. The entire length of the valley and slopes of the surrounding mountains were covered in terraces, as this fertile place has been cultivating life giving crops since prehistoric times. The occupants of the holy valley live a life that has changed little over the millennia and they could be seen out working their fields according to their ancient customs. There was very little machinery to be seen here and it seemed that these people lived their lives much as their ancestors had.

The train ride had a surreal feeling and indeed the rest of my time in the Andes would prove to have a dreamlike quality. The San Pedro ceremony had enlightened me in a way that still lingers to this day. The Father medicine of the Incas had renewed a childlike wonder of the world for me. It was almost like a paradigm had shifted for me and I was looking at the world from a different and more peaceful place. I was seeing things that I would have ignored before. Things that I would have passed over in my seemingly frantic previous life now were demanding my attention. It seemed to me like my life had slowed down a notch. My rush to see and do as much as I could in my time allowed had been replaced by a yearning to know and appreciate the things that I had time to see. It was not until later, when I had time to reflect, that I realized that the ceremony had given me a life changing gift! My operation had given me a newfound love for life, but the San Pedro had altered my perspective. I now knew what it was to live each moment as if it was all there was. I could now fully appreciate all the marvels that make up our daily lives. I would now actually take the time to see what was happening all around me. All the little things that we take for granted that make up our world. The life-giving warmth of the sun! The kiss of a cool breeze. The chirps of the birds and the buzz of the insects! The gift that the medicine had given me was the ability to live in the moment. This was the first, but not the only gift that this enchanting land of the Incas would impart to me!

~•~

Aguas Calientes was the way station to Machu Picchu and, as such, it consisted mostly of hotels and restaurants catering to the hordes of tourists that flocked to Machu Picchu each year. There was also a hot spring and a huge marketplace. The market seemed endless and offered everything a tourist could possibly want. The restaurants offered a wide variety and the streets had a laid-back vibe. No matter where I went, there was always music of one sort or another in the air. I felt very comfortable here.

We had arrived early in the day and after a leisurely lunch Tatyana suggested a hike to a nearby waterfall. What I liked about this tour group was that, when we weren't traveling or in ceremony, our time was our own. So, while some of the group elected to stay and explore the town, a group of us took a sightseeing hike along the river that meandered through the valley. I had been in many forests before but had never experienced a high mountain tropical forest. The plant life was diverse and spectacularly unfamiliar to me! There were broad-leafed plants, creeping vines and flowering trees that I had never seen before. The terrain off the trail was rugged and dense and I could see why the Incas had needed their extensive highway system, as traversing this mountain jungle or the rocky crags of the Andes would be otherwise impossible.

We were hot and tired by the time we reached the hidden waterfall. This was June, wintertime in Peru, and we were at 8,000 feet but the weather was still balmy. The water was cold, but the lure of the beautiful waterfall proved too powerful and several of my intrepid young companions could not resist the call of the falls. The clear blue waters tumbling from the dense green jungle seemed impossibly majestic and I imagined that this must have been a holy place for the Incas.

The sun was waning by the time we returned to town and I was exhausted. The altitude and exercise had taken their toll and I found I could hardly keep my eyes open to eat my supper. I beat a hasty retreat to my room and was surprised to find it hard to fall asleep. My excitement for tomorrow's expedition won out over my drowsiness and I lay there for quite a while before succumbing to dreams of the Flying City of Machu Picchu!

~•~

If I had it to do over I would hike the Incan trail that led from the river up to the mountain summit where Machu Picchu hid among the clouds. Heights are not my strong suit, but to climb up to the hidden citadel on the ancient Incan Highway seemed a more fitting way to approach such a holy place. The near vertical trail and the thin air would probably have been my undoing, and I was probably fortunate that there was a steady stream of busses ferrying visitors to the site. Our group piled in an old school bus and we rode up the too narrow dirt-track full of switchbacks that had me looking anywhere but down.

The entrance to the ruins was filled with busses divesting themselves of hordes of confused looking tourists. The hectic vibe of the place was aggravated by would-be guides hawking their services in a myriad of languages. I was a bit taken aback. The crowds were in contrast to my expectations of the mystical citadel. I wasn't prepared for this mass of humanity!

My angst vanished as soon as I passed through the gates and had my first glimpse of the ancient city perched precariously atop the seemingly inaccessible mountain peak. The fortress was surrounded by jungle-shrouded peaks that appeared and dissolved through the veil of ever shifting clouds. It gave the impression of motion and I could see why some called it the Flying City. This was one place that was untouched by the destruction wrought by the Spaniards as they had never thought to look to the skies!

I was stunned and frozen in place as a palpable wave of spiritual energy broke over me. The feeling of wonder and awe that had overwhelmed me at The Temple of the Moon came back in full force now. If the Sacred Valley was a vast open-aired cathedral, then this was the Sistine Chapel floating in the heavens! I was humbled and inspired by this place of power. It was surely the most beautiful place on earth! I had no intention of ever leaving.

I slowly became self-aware again and realized I was blocking the path and had, in a matter of minutes, lost my companions. Once past the gate the crowds thinned out as paths took off in several different directions. In a way, I was relieved, because I do my best exploring on my own.

The sheer size and condition of the mountain fortress stunned me! I could see why this place was considered one of the Seven Wonders of the World! The citadel was surrounded and supported by more than 600 terraces. The terraces were marvels of engineering. They not only served as a foundation for the massive stone complex, they provided food and controlled erosion from the 80 inches of rain a year!

The terraces that connected the sprawling site are the main reason why the 500 year old ruins are in such pristine shape. The Flying City looked almost as if it had just been abandoned! The architecture was incredibly intact save for the thatched roofs which had long since succumbed to the humid climate. I climbed one of the many stone staircases that connected the sprawling sanctuary. Machu Picchu consisted of around 150 buildings and many temples. There was running water and 14 fountains. At its height the city housed 500-1000 people of nobility. Most believe that Machu Picchu was a religious center, observatory and retreat for kings! A place of worship and learning. And I had but an afternoon to explore this place that had haunted my dreams since childhood.

It was an incredible day and the air was crisp and thin. The ancient site floated above the clouds, and the sun warmed the granite buildings that were arrayed on the mountain top. The temperature was perfect, and it was a fantastic day for adventure! I wandered from one amazement to the next and I realized that this place was even more remarkable than my dreams. I sometimes would find myself spell-bound by the incredible craftsmanship of the massive stone walls or the extraordinary way the architects incorporated the living bedrock of the mountain into their construction. Again, the skill of the builders was almost beyond comprehension, the stones fitting together seamlessly, without mortar, and surviving intact for hundreds of years.

I was beginning to realize that the strange affinity I had for the ruins in Arizona extended here to Peru. The truth being that I had never been moved by any place the way this mystical fortress stirred me! I had no plan worked out to explore the site and let my instincts guide me. The complex was simply spectacular, but there were four places that were especially provoking.

The Temple of the Condor drew me like a magnet and left me astonished. This open-aired temple is the most breathtaking example of the ingenious Incan art of stone masonry. The floors of the temple and of all the buildings were carved out of the bedrock of the granite mountainside. They were perfectly flat and burnished by use. Protruding from the floor, also carved out of the bedrock, was an altar in the shape of a condor's head and neck feathers. On the wall behind the altar, the master craftsmen had skillfully shaped the natural rock into the outspread wings of a condor. The overall impression was a 3-dimensional visage of a majestic condor in flight! The stark beauty and celestial atmosphere of the temple transfixed me! I almost reluctantly continued my explorations.

I roamed through a maze of exquisitely crafted structures, my imagination running amuck trying to envision their purposes and the extraordinary people that had made them. When I entered The Temple of the Sun, I was again moved by the powerful sense of mysticism! It was obviously a very sacred place. Again, an altar rose from the floor and there was an impressive semi-circular outer wall. The temple was used for religious and scientific purposes. Set in the wall were windows that aligned with the summer and winter solstices. The ancient priests were also scientists who used astrology to better understand and live in harmony with nature. Science and religion were one and the same for these sages of long ago. Their wisdom seemed at once more primitive and more advanced. My empathy with these people was strong!

The temple of the Mirror Pools did nothing to diminish my respect. As with the altars, these pools rose from the bedrock of the mountain. They were perfect semi-circles that, when filled with water, transformed into unmoving mirrors of the sky above. By peering into these pools, the ancient scientists could track the passage of the sun in the day and the constellations at night. The Incas had a superb sense of their place in the universe and had a vast complex of observatories of which Machu Picchu was the center. As I stared into the pools, I could see the sun above perfectly and without blinding myself. I was entranced and would have spent all day there if not for the many other people waiting to get a chance to peer into the mirrored skies.

The nearby Intiwatana Sundial was further evidence of the Incan reverence for astrology. In the Quechuan language of the Incas, Intiwatana means "where the sun is tied down." The sundial also rises magically from the bedrock and is the largest of its kind in the world. The four sides of the massive granite tool align perfectly with the four cardinal points. It is quite likely that the scholars who lived in Machu Picchu knew more about the heavens above than did their conquerors.

After hours of climbing endless staircases I started to get tired and a bit light-headed from the thin mountain air. I had explored most of the vast fortress and was beginning to tire of the crowds. I began to search for someplace I could relax by myself and just revel in the ethereal energy that this place of knowledge and spirituality emitted.

I spotted a doorway at the end of a hall that seemed to open to nothing. As I neared the opening I realized that this truly was a door to nowhere. Beyond the portal there were a couple of terraces and then a shear drop obscured by clouds. The way was roped off, but I was never a big fan of rules. I climbed over the rope and skirted the wall until I found a likely niche and sat with my back to the ancient university. It was almost deafeningly quiet out here away from the others! Occasionally the clouds below would break, and I would catch a glimpse of a stunning jungle gorge and river far below.

In the church-like silence I was extremely aware of my breath. The thin air tasted especially sweet to me! With each breath I could feel the rarified air enriching the blood cells in my lungs. In a moment of clarity, I realized just how precious each breath was. With each inhalation I was receiving the gift of life from Mother Earth, or Pachamama, as the Incas called her in Quechuan. For the first time in my life I pondered just how miraculous this life-giving process was!

As I sat marveling at the simple act of breathing, I became aware of a slight vibration. The earth beneath me and even the wall at my back were emitting the slightest of oscillations. I thought it was surely my imagination, but the tiny pulsations didn't diminish. Instinctively, I began trying to sync my breath with the vibrating earth. For a time, that was all that existed for me. My breath melding with the frequency of the earth! For a fleeting instant, I felt that I knew my place in the universe and I, for the briefest of times, I knew complete harmony in my world.

I gradually noticed a slight change in the air and looked up to see the sun was about to plunge behind a nearby mountaintop. Damn! How long had I been sitting there? I scrambled back over the rope and entered a nearly deserted fortress. I was a bit bewildered, as I realized that I had lost some time out there perched on the mountainside! I was calm and felt revitalized despite the fact I seemed to have missed last call! I ambled back through the Flying City and now, as the light began to dim, I was treated with visages of the proud and superior people who once called this place home. I caught glimpses of magnificently adorned priests and priestesses going about their lives steeped in ceremony and enlightenment. These were people who knew and lived their lives in a state of harmony that has been lost to the rest of us.

I was relieved to see people of more substance gathered about the gate. They turned out to be workers waiting for the last bus. They looked amused but not too surprised to see a gringo who had lost track of time.

As I approached, one called out jokingly, "Señor, looks like you missed your bus!"

"Lo siento," I replied. "Que tan lejos esta la ciudad?" I am sorry. How far is it to town?

"Only ten miles." he said laughingly.

"Ok. Gracias." I was unfazed. I had just had the best day of my life! I wasn't too worried about a long hike back. I started down the dirt road.

"Espere, señor." He cried out. "I was joking! A bus is coming. You can have a ride with us."

I thoroughly enjoyed the ride back to town with the jovial workers who laughed and sang the whole way. I was ever more grateful as I came to the realization that hiking down the mountain in the dark would not have been fun.

As I reflected on a perfect day, I wondered about the time I had lost while resting against the wall on the mountainside. How totally in sync I had been with nature! That was to be a lasting gift from the majestic City in the Clouds. I had the realization that she had given me the gift of meditation! I had tried many times before and had always failed miserably. I could never clear my mind.

This, my second gift from the land of the Incas, was the ability to focus on my breathing and feel the vibration of the earth around me. From that day forward, I was able to use the memory of that moment outside the walls of Machu Picchu when I connected with my breath to the very earth to focus and clear my mind. Again, I felt like I had experienced a paradigm shift. I couldn't wait to try again. I was excited and grateful and eager to begin. To this day, I try to greet the sun in the morning and put him to sleep in the evening, with a moment of quiet reflection which inevitably involves of memory of that day outside the walls!

We took the train back to Cusco and had one last dinner as a group. For the bright, fun-loving group of young people who had already been to the Amazon, the tour was over. They would all be going separate ways, back to their homes or to continue their adventures. I could truly say that I would miss them. I wished that they would go back with us to the jungle. I never would have guessed that I would have made such a connection with them. This tour was exceeding my expectations in almost every way! We said our goodbyes and exchanged our info and promises to keep in touch.

There would be six of us plus Tatyana catching an early morning flight to Iquitos, the largest Peruvian city on the Amazon. From there we would go to the remote Arkana retreat at the headwaters of the Amazon to begin the real reason that most of us had come on this tour. Each of us had spent considerable time and money to get here. Each of us had their own reason for coming this great distance to experience the plant medicine called Ayahuasca, the great Mother medicine of the Peruvians.

I had taken every opportunity to question the previous group about their experiences and I was a little concerned. Although each of them had said that they had been very satisfied with the results, they had described very different, intense and often painful ceremonies. In my research I had learned that the plant Mother would almost invariably make the participant confront their most painful memories. They told me that this was not an easy thing to do and harder on some than others. Some of the group were trying to overcome emotional traumas and would be forced to relive them. This was an aspect of how the medicine worked. Through realizing and facing their fears, most people were able to move past their issues.

I had a healthy respect for my companions as they had come here to willingly to face their past and worst memories. I felt that it took a special person to make that kind of sacrifice and I was coming to the conclusion that my companions were indeed very special people, each in their own way! My reasons for coming had more to do with my health issues. While my childhood had not been marred by trauma and I didn't think I carried around a lot of emotional baggage, I had done little preparation for delving into and reliving my past. I was beginning to wonder what I had got myself into.

Chapter Five
Mother Ayahuasca

In 1880 Iquitos was a sleepy enclave in the vast Amazon basin surrounded by almost impenetrable endless jungle. It had been founded a hundred years earlier by Jesuits as a base for their religious missions into the heart of the Amazon.

The simple life of the indigenous people of the jungle was shattered when one of the native tree's sap was found to have an amazing elasticity. The result was an invasion of Europeans and the birth of the Rubber Boom. For the people of the region this brought near slavery conditions and catastrophic disease. The horrific conditions relented when industrious merchants smuggled out the seeds of the rubber trees and began cultivating them in a more accessible location in Asia.

By this time, the peaceful village had been transformed into a bustling port city. To this day, it is the biggest city in the world that is not accessible by road. Today nearly half a million people are trying to eke out a living in one of the poorest regions of Peru. The poverty is slowly being alleviated by a growing tourism industry for those looking to explore the wonders of the rainforest. It is also becoming known around the world as a center for those interested in the ancient shamanic ways of plant healing. The most popular of these medicinal plants, and my reason for this quest, is the Mother plant, Ayahuasca.

Because the city is reachable only by air or a 2,200-mile boat trip up the Amazon, there are few automobiles. The streets are dominated by motorcycles and some 50,000 motorized rickshaws which results in what seems to be a rather loud and chaotic free-for-all.

In contrast to the cool clean air of Cusco, Iquitos greeted us with heat and humidity. It was 75 degrees and sticky and my decision to come in the winter months was reinforced. I couldn't imagine what it would be like in the heat of summer or the rainy season.

Tatyana guided us to a line of dubious looking rickshaws which could hold two people and had a luggage rack in back. Our ride to the hostel was a manic dash in which our driver miraculously wove through a multitude of motorcycles, other rickshaws and close encounters with the occasional bus. The city was loud and frenzied and filled with exhaust fumes. I had a sigh of relief when the driver skidded to a halt in front of our hostel. Tatyana got us checked in, gave us a quick rundown on the local restaurants and attractions, and we were on our own. She instructed us to meet the next morning at a small café on the Malecon, which was a Riverwalk overlooking the river and not far from the hostel.

Not one to hide out in the hotel, I stowed my gear and headed out to explore. I was met at the door by a host of street vendors selling everything you could imagine and some things that you couldn't. Their wares were interesting, but I knew enough about traveling that I was not going to buy anything without looking around. These street hawkers were much more aggressive than those in Cusco. I was moved by their plight. These were hardworking and obviously somewhat desperate people who were doing their best to provide for their families. Unfortunately, I was not in the market for souvenirs as I had only brought so much money and I was struggling with the bags I already had.

After a bit, I was able to get through the trinket bearing mob and I made a dash for the main square. To my chagrin, one of the young peddlers was keeping pace with me! When I was sure we were clear of the others, I slowed down and turned to my persistent entrepreneur.

He was a good-looking, smiling and vital young man and he announced in near perfect English, "I am your personal guide and you would be foolish not to let me show you around."

I had to explain to him that I was not the typical rich tourist and was traveling on a budget. He was undaunted.

"Ah. You are here to meet the Mother. Good. I can take you to my village. We have the best shaman. He will cure you," he answered.

I explained to him that I was already part of a tour group and we were going to a retreat tomorrow. He introduced himself as Jimmy and he gave me a stern lecture about how the "tour groups" were taking over and he could take me to an authentic shaman. He seemed a bit bitter about the foreigners coming in and investing in Ayahuasca retreats. He said they were making a mockery of the Peruvian beliefs and taking advantage of the sacred Mother plant. Besides that, he said that they took the profits and gave very little in return. When he learned which tour group I was with he relented a little, saying that they were one of the better retreats and that I would be all right with them. I had heard that it can be very dangerous to come and seek out an Ayahuasca ceremony on your own. This was a primitive and lawless region that was largely influenced by the drug trade. I was content with the safety of the group and the reputation of the people running it, but I could understand Jimmy's sentiments. I could understand why these proud, but impoverished people, did not want to have their traditions and beliefs taken advantage of by foreigners.

I told Jimmy how much I was willing to shell out for a short walking tour and he readily agreed. He fell back into the relaxed and easygoing demeanor that I had come to expect of these young Peruvians. I soon came to respect Jimmy's intellect, his knowledge of history and his obvious passion for his people and the environment. I ended up feeling encouraged for the next generation of Peru. They seemed at once carefree and fierce in their determination to preserve their culture and heritage and the amazing country that has been left in their charge. Another advantage of walking with him was that I seemed to be immune from the other aggressive street merchants due to his presence and some unwritten street hawkers' code.

Jimmy took me down to the Belen floating market. It was a huge open-aired market built on stilts that was flooded for much of the year! The biggest of its kind in hundreds of miles, this was the center of commerce for the peoples of the Upper Amazonian basin. People came from all over the jungle using the only mode of transportation, the riverboat. Along with them came dancing and music and food of every type under the sun. The vast jungle river system was home to an ecosystem that was totally exotic to me. The market was an endless display of sights and smells and humanity that was almost overwhelming. My favorite part was the herbal and medicinal plants section. I could have spent days there learning about the thousands of plants and herbs and medicines that were the gifts of the jungle. The aromas were tangible, and there was a pungent flavor to the air.

After my too brief visit to the vibrant bazaar we walked up the Riverwalk while Jimmy talked animatedly about his city, the rain-forest, his country, and his plans for their future. As we walked, Jimmy pointed out the café where my group was to meet the next morning. This portion of the riverbank was beautifully maintained and sported shops and restaurants and a partying atmosphere. The view of the huge river that was the life-blood of the city was mesmerizing to say the least. To me, the mighty river seemed to be a huge living and immensely powerful creature. I was humbled by its sheer size and majesty, and this was the dry season! I tried but failed to picture this behemoth swelled by months of rain. This was the life-giving and all-powerful matriarch of the Amazon jungle and her ways were far beyond my understanding.

Jimmy pointed me towards an Ayahuasca friendly eatery overlooking the river and he bid me good luck in my ceremonies. He was off to pursue his dreams and other likely tourists. As per the instructions from Pulse Tours, I had been adhering to a strict diet in an attempt to cleanse my body in preparation for my upcoming Ayahuasca encounter. The medicine was said to purge your body of toxins and the fewer you had going in, the fewer needed to come out. It was also a way to demonstrate your intent and respect for the plant and the ceremony.

As I ate, I watched an elaborate production of some kind on the Malecon featuring outlandish costumes, frenetic dancing and lots of music and laughter. Although I could make no sense of it, I was once again amazed by the people's zest for life and their unabated love of the festival. Like Cusco, for having so little, they also appeared to have very full and happy lives.

As I walked back to my hostel down an unfamiliar road in a faraway place, I would have been lying to say that I wasn't having second thoughts. I reexamined my motives and weighed them against the risks. I had come seeking healing and a way to live with my new limitations, but I knew that I was also looking for something else. I could just not put it to words. I also knew that forays into the Amazon jungle were not without inherent dangers. Whatever the risks/rewards, I was committed now, and I was never one to look back. I was determined to see this through. I spent an uneasy night in a warm room where the ceiling fan offered little relief. I vowed to upgrade to a room with air conditioning if it was in my cards to make the return trip from the jungle.

I was sitting outside at the appointed café, enjoying a fruit bowl for breakfast, when the rest of our group started showing up for our meeting in the morning. It turned out that we were also meeting a new group of eight more people who were headed to the retreat. I was fascinated to meet them and to hear what had brought them this long distance to share this adventure with me. They were mostly in their twenties or thirties and it appeared that I was again to be the eldest. I noticed a difference between this group and the group in Cusco who had already done their Ayahuasca ceremonies. The previous group had been carefree and happy and acted as close as family. The new group was friendly and looked as excited as I was to begin our quest, but they sat in small groups and talked quietly. I could sense that everyone was a bit antsy about our trek up the Amazon and our Ayahuasca ceremonies to come. I couldn't help but wonder if we would emerge from the rain forest as a family as had the others.

Tatyana worked her organizing miracles and soon we were crammed into two more vans and weaving through the virtual insanity that was Iquitos' traffic. We took the only road out of the city and drove nearly two hours to the port of Nauta. The port was situated at the confluence of two great rivers, the Maranon and the Ucayali, which met to form the mighty Amazon. Nauta was a cacophony of sight, sounds and smells as this was the main way station for the bounty of jungle goods headed to the Belen market in Iquitos.

It took all of Tatyana's considerable skills to navigate the group and our gear through the maze of bustling mass of humanity that was Nauta. There was an incredible amount of energy here as these poor, but industrious people went about the tribulations of living in the Amazon basin. This was a fascinating view of unadulterated life in the jungle and I was distracted at every turn. With patience and determination, Tatyana somehow kept us on point and we reached the river's bank with our bags intact and not a single casualty.

We loaded into two long, thin river boats with covered roofs that I heard called "peche peche." We settled in for a two-hour boat ride to the Arkana retreat far up the massive Ucayali River.

I was a bit surprised when an armed policeman joined us in the boat. When I asked Tatyana about him she said that he was here to deter river pirates. She explained that the river was a highway for drug traffickers who weren't above pillaging the occasional tourist boat. As we left the last vestiges of civilization, the realization of just how vulnerable we were, began to sink in. There were no restaurants, television or hospitals where we were headed.

The boat ride was surreal, and I felt extremely blessed to be able to experience the wonders of the massive river and the great jungle. Believe me when I say, that documentaries do not hold a candle to the real thing! We were scrutinized by pink river dolphins and yelled at by monkeys and parrots. Every so often we could see alligators lounging on the banks in the sun. Occasionally, we would catch sight of a small fishing village and we would get a glimpse of what life was really like for the people of the jungle.

It was a long trek up the river and in between the sights I found time to reflect. What a strange turn my life had taken on that rainy morning in Bisbee. By this time, I had accepted the fact that I had been called to Peru by the Mother plant Ayahuasca. This had been a hard pill for me to swallow, as it entailed personifying a plant. Not only that, but I was admitting that she had a conscience and the mystical ability to reach out to a rather mundane person in a faraway country. This was a leap for me. The people that I had talked with who had had the privilege of having done an Ayahuasca ceremony were often unable to put it to words. Their accounts were fantastical and varied and inevitably beyond my comprehension. I had no doubt that I was heading down a road, or a river, that was about to change my life as I knew it. I realized that I had not been overly impressed with my previous life and that I welcomed the change. I was also aware that I was at once excited and terrified. I was leaving my old self behind as we motored up this exotic river into the unknown.

~•~

I was feeling cramped, and the sun and humidity were beginning to wear me down, when we pulled up to a small wooden pier. On the banks above was a compound of thatched roofed buildings on stilts. The river was what seemed like a mile wide at this point. Given that the buildings were a good ten feet above the banks, I could only imagine what a ten-foot rise in the water level would mean. The whole jungle would basically turn into a huge swamp in the rainy season. Again, I was glad of the timing of my trip. With an occasional afternoon shower to break the heat, the weather was idyllic. My doctor had supplied me with a pill regimen to ward off malaria and I had come armed with a near lethal array of insect repellant.

There were two buildings divided up into cabins for sleeping, a workout room, kitchen and eating area and several bathrooms with showers attached. Dominating the other structures was a large round open-aired building called a Maloca, where the ceremonies were held. We were assigned sleeping quarters and told to meet back in the Maloca.

There were three bunks covered in mosquito netting in my cabin. It was small, clean and simple and I would find that we would spend little time there. The whole compound was neat and well maintained by a work force from a nearby village. The cheerful way that they went about their simple, but grueling lives would have a profound effect on me. They endured what we would consider extreme poverty with a constant smile, a ready joke, or spontaneous song. The lessons I learned from them about living in grace with few material possessions would not be lost on me.

The Maloca was an impressive structure built with sacred geometry and as I entered it felt much like entering a church or any other holy place. The circular temple's walls were open to the air but screened in to protect occupants from the voracious insects of the jungle. Arrayed around the perimeter were mats for comfort and I choose one and set down to wait for the others. As I waited, I was hypnotized by the elaborate beam-work supporting the thatched roof. When the others had filed in and selected a mat we all sat in a circle and started to get to know each other. We were all from different demographics, but we shared English as a common language.

When we were situated, Tatyana entered followed by a couple of young women that she introduced as facilitators. They were here to assist us in our upcoming ceremonies, as our individual journeys could be quite confusing, emotionally taxing and physically demanding. We would find that the Mother Ayahuasca worked in mysterious ways. These attractive young women were very special and obviously chosen for their compassion and empathy. During the next week they would spend hours helping us understand and talking us through all the awkward and embarrassing things that inevitably come up while working with the plant Mother. We had all done our research and we knew that Ayahuasca ceremonies could be demanding. Once committed to a ceremony there would be no turning back. These pretty women were like our personal psychiatrists, and I was to be amazed by their kindness and professionalism. I was also grateful for their respect for the traditions and for the ceremony. In the next few days I was to have a kind of spiritual awakening and the ceremonies were a huge part of my experience. I was starting to understand why Ayahuasca was an integral part of these peoples' religion.

Once we were all seated there were about 20 of us in the circle. Tatyana started by a quick does and don'ts of the retreat. She told us a bit about herself and introduced her staff. Then she asked if everyone else would do the same. As the young women of her staff talked about themselves I realized that they were all vibrant, clearheaded and clearly very intelligent. They had all participated in many Ayahuasca ceremonies and were plainly none the worse for it. If anything, they seemed to be on a slightly higher level of awareness than the rest of us. Each of them had that certain glow about them that I had first noticed with the group I met in Cusco. This was reassuring to me as one of the questions about working with the plant Mother was, if I could expect any negative long-term side-effects.

As we worked our way around the circle, I was amazed by the variety of reasons that had drawn us all to the remote jungle at that place and time. I was impressed by my companions and couldn't have picked a finer group if I had tried. As we talked, I came to the conclusion that although we came from different places and cultures we all had something in common. We were all facing our fears and living our dreams. I marveled at the courage of my young friends and was proud to be one of the group. When it came around to me, I told my story and how I thought I had been called to come here in a dream. I was stunned to learn that this was not uncommon at all. In fact, I got the impression that each of us had been called in some way and was slightly amazed to be here. I remember thinking that my life was about to take a huge turn and I wasn't quite sure in which direction. If I wanted to back out, this was my last chance. There was one thing I had always known about myself. I was no quitter. I hadn't come all this way to chicken out.

After our introductions Tatyana said there were to be two different ceremonies offered today. Both were thought to help prepare for the first Ayahuasca ceremony which would be held the next evening. Ayahuasca ceremonies were traditionally held at night. While San Pedro is related to the Sun and the Father, Ayahuasca was related to the Moon and the Mother. Whether or not we wanted to be included in any ceremony was up to us, but if these would help prepare me for my Ayahuasca ceremony, then I was going to participate.

The first ceremony was a "Kambo" ritual performed by a local shaman. Kambo is a secretion from a giant monkey frog. It is a powerful medicine used to increase strength and stamina. It is also used to prevent malaria, infections, and a myriad of other health problems. The medicine is scraped off the back of the frog onto sticks and dried and must be absorbed into the bloodstream. The shaman lights a small stick similar to an incense stick on fire to get a coal going. He then quickly burns through two or three layers of skin on the patient's upper arm. The secretion is then rubbed into the burn. The sting is not very painful and goes away quickly. When it came my turn, the shaman burned me three times very quickly and rubbed in the balm.

I retreated to my mat and looked about to see how the others reacted to their treatments. Only about half of the group was game to try this and one woman had a bad reaction when her face swelled up. The swelling was temporary, thank goodness, and she was better after soaking her head in a bucket of water and lying down for a bit. As for myself, I felt queasy for about a half-hour and then it eased away with no other real effects. The medicine takes days to realize the benefits, so it is hard to say if I benefitted at all. To be honest, I wasn't real impressed, but then, I had no idea what long-term benefits I might receive.

In the second ceremony the shaman offered a plant medicine called "Nunu." Tatyana obviously liked this one, as she volunteered to be the first. This medicine's primary ingredient is tobacco but it also consists of dried macambo nut, cacao as well as bark and leaves of other medicinal plants ground into a fine powder. It is said to clear and heal the sinuses and the pituitary gland. It was to cleanse and relax us, and open us up for our upcoming Ayahuasca ceremony. The shaman loaded the concoction into the end of a two-foot long hollow reed. Tatyana guided one end into her nostril and the shaman blew on the other end sending the medicine into her sinuses. She then repeated on the other side.

When it came to be my turn, the effects of this remarkable medicine were instantaneous and startling. I felt as if the top of my head had been removed and cold clear air was flowing in. It was as if I had been given a new set of unused sinuses and the slightly rotten odor of the huge river and vast jungle was almost overwhelming. I had a brief revelation about how rich and full life must be for my dog Chapo and I realized how underused my sense of smell was. I had an overwhelming urge to explore and experience this incredible place.

I wandered down to the boat dock and sat with my feet dangling in the cool, muddy waters. I considered the wonders of this foreign land. The sun was relentless but balanced by the coolness of the water and a warm breeze. The air was alive with the sounds of mysterious birds and the shrieks of troops of monkeys swinging through the trees. From the water, came the gasps of surfacing river porpoises and the occasional bark of an alligator. In the background, I could hear laughter and conversation from my companions and snatches of song from the villagers as they went happily about their business.

I closed my eyes and listened to my breathing and took in all the smells and sounds. I was swept up and carried away by the breeze. I stepped outside of myself and saw the powerful forces of nature that made up the Amazon. For a time, I was able to set aside my ego and was able to just "be." I was surrounded by a myriad of miracles, and for a fleeting moment, I felt in sync with the elements and Mother Nature, or Pachamama, in a way I never had before.

The sun had set, and the camp was quiet by the time I made my way to my room. Most of my fellow explorers were in the Maloca involved in quiet conversations. I imagined that they were feeling as anxious about tomorrow as I was. I decided to forgo their companionship in favor of rest as I had a feeling I would be needing it.

~•~

The next morning some of us went on an amazing guided jungle trek. There was also a workout room and a yoga class to pass the time. Ayahuasca ceremonies are held in the dark, so I spent my afternoon trying to mentally prepare myself for the evening's ordeal. I failed miserably and, if anything, only managed to increase my uneasiness. I consoled myself with the thought that I was about to have a possibly life changing experience and I was not a coward for feeling apprehensive.

Around dusk we all gathered and cleansed ourselves for the ceremony with a floral bath which consisted of dumping a bucket of water filled with flower petals over our heads. It was refreshing and smelled good and I entered the Maloca with flower petals in my hair.

On one side of the circle, clouded in an inevitable haze of smoke, sat Shaman Wiler and his wife Angela. Mapacho is a kind of jungle tobacco that is considered a sacred medicine. Our shaman was a big believer in the plants' power and as we faced him in the waning light of dusk, he seemed shrouded in a mystical fog. The shaman and his wife seemed to be very happy, easygoing people. They had much the same temperament as shaman Luis in Cusco. Shaman Wiler seemed much larger and commanded more respect inside the Maloca than when I had seen him outside. Sixteen adventurous souls entered the somber Maloca and the air was highly charged with the atmosphere of ceremony. We each chose a mat and sat in a large circle facing the shaman and Tatyana made the introductions.

For most of us this was to be our first ceremony with the Mother Ayahuasca but scattered about were a few people who had experience with the plant Mother. Tatyana and a handful of facilitators were to abstain and were here to help with the flow of the ceremony and to give aid to anyone who might become distressed. The respect for the ceremony and tradition shown by these facilitators were a huge part of the success of this retreat. They were intelligent, caring and empathetic guides and we were to be lucky to have them.

In the waning sunlight the Shaman Wiler called each of us up to sit with him. He asked our intentions and judged how much of the plant medicine was to be given.

He was also here to guide us in our ceremony. He did this primarily with songs called Icaros. He used these songs to guide us to the places that he thought we needed to go. As in all things, there were good shamans and not so good shamans. Our shaman sang his Icaros with the help of his wife and together they sang in a particularly beautiful and powerful harmony. After determining how much of the plant medicine was needed, he poured a thick looking black concoction from a jug into a cup. I thanked him for the medicine and his guidance and drank down what had to be the vilest tasting brew known to man! My first instinct was to throw it up on the spot, but I managed to retreat to my mat without making a mess.

It was dark by the time the Shaman Wiler finished dispersing the foul-tasting medicine. The participants were led to the shaman and back to their mats by the facilitators who used small flashlights when necessary. In the darkness I could hear some of the others begin to purge themselves of the medicine into buckets that had been provided for this purpose.

I also began to feel queasy and before I knew it, I was contributing to my bucket. I started to lose contact with what was happening around me and I retreated inward in the darkness. One thing I would be aware of this night and that was the location of my bucket. My bucket and I would become fast friends this evening.

I could not see much in the darkness of the Maloca. It was getting harder to keep my eyes open and I was aware that the guy next to me was not doing so well. He was to cry and moan all through the coming ceremony and it was almost like I could feel his pain. In the darkness of the Maloca I could see nothing. The shamans had begun to sing a rhythmic Icaro that had an immediate effect on me. Their chanting was haunting and persuasive, and as soon as I closed my eyes, it seemed to lift me off my mat and hurl me into time and space. I flew through a kaleidoscope of swirling colors that must be akin to entering a wormhole.

I found myself deposited in a typical Peruvian village with dirt roads and stucco buildings. This was unlike any dream I had ever had. I was fully conscious and had all my faculties. I was an active participant and not so much the spectator that was my usual role in my dreams. The intricate detail of the pueblo was something far too extensive for my dreaming mind to conjure. I felt the dirt between my toes and tasted the dust in my mouth.

I followed the dirt road through town and was immediately aware that there was something weird about the place. It was deserted, silent and unmistakably eerie. As I walked down the road the light seemed to be fading, and time seemed to be warping as the pueblo morphed into a modern, but lifeless city. I kept moving and the buildings changed to abandoned warehouses and dark factories. Soon I was surrounded by a maze of huge valves and pistons and conveyor belts. It was loud now and hot and it smelled of diesel and oil. This place was a steam-punks dream, but to me, it was never-ending and oppressive. I began to panic. It seemed there was no way out!

I was aware of a voice. It was calm and alluring and as I followed it I left the grinding machinery behind and swam back through the wormhole and into the familiar setting of the Maloca. I was sitting on my mat and one of the facilitators was whispering to me. She took my hand and led me in the dark to kneel in front of the Shaman Wiler. He began to sing an Icaro that was meant for me only. I was hypnotized by his powerful bass voice and was entranced by the alto of his wife Angela's chant. It seemed to lilt like a butterfly through his forcible song. This ritual, which had been enacted for thousands of years, was deeply moving. After their Icaro the shaman circled me blowing smoke from his Mapacho and spitting some cheap smelling cologne on my head. It was the exact scene I had dreamt about on that rainy night in Arizona! I was actually living my dream! With that revelation I had an epiphany. I saw clearly that there is no such thing as fate or coincidence. There are only infinite possibilities and that our very lives are dreams that we can manifest, much as I was manifesting my dream from Arizona.

I was led back to my mat and settled in. My companion next to me was still moaning and crying. It was beginning to wear on me. I tried to get him to stop. I continued to purge. I urged my neighbor to please just stop for a few moments, I didn't think I could take much more of his pain. At one point he was thrashing around and landed on top of me. His struggle was beginning to overwhelm me and I thought I might be sucked into his nightmare. To my great relief a heavenly voice was whispering my name and asked me if I would like to move to another mat.

A gentle hand guided me across the room, bucket in hand, and I settled onto a different mat. The moaning was still echoing, but was not as intense. As soon as I closed my eyes I was falling. I fell for what seemed like an eternity through the darkness and into the depths of my soul. Finally, I came to rest in a place deep within myself where I had never had the courage to go before. I seemed to be in a hall made of mirror-like black obsidian. There was only one direction to go, but I was frozen in place by terror. I knew instinctively that this was a place that was full of things that I did not want to meet. Indeed, this was a place full of things that I had spent my whole life avoiding. I was in that secret little box that we all have where we store the things that are too painful for us to face. Fear gripped me, and I felt I was suffocating. With no other options, I took a tentative step down the hall. With each step, as I peered into the black mirror walls, I was assaulted by every lie, every misdeed, and every act of selfishness or ego that I had ever committed in my long life. And the list was endless! Amazingly, with each of the unwanted memories came a complete understanding of the instance. For every lie, I understood the underlying reason for the lie and all the ramifications that it had caused. These were stark truths of which there was no denying! With the full understanding of the causes and effects of the offending memory came the ability to accept it for what it was. These were memories that lay festering in the dark and, once brought into the open and acknowledged, they would fade away and I would be confronted by the next one lurking in the mirror.

The Mother was ruthless in her thoroughness and brutal in her honesty. There was no hiding anything from her. Although I could feel resolution, the process was brutal and grueling and seemingly without end. I felt as if I was drowning and this was where I would die. Here, among all my misdeeds. Just when I had resigned myself to having lived a horrible life and having been condemned to an eternity of re-living it, I became aware of bits of conversation, some crying, and some laughter. The glue that was holding me in this dark place began to weaken and I was able to break free of my dismal dungeon. I began to ascend through the darkness towards a distant light. It was like swimming up from the depths of the ocean, seeing the light of the sun, but never reaching the surface.

Finally, with a gasp, I broke through the surface and into the Maloca. The shamans had stopped their powerful Icaros and a few candles were being lit. Some of the others were stirring and coming around to the present. Others were still obviously in the throes of their journey. There was some giddiness, but mostly it was a somber and respectful atmosphere. From the looks on my fellow adventurer's faces, I could tell that they all had been on an incredible journey! Some were eager to talk about it, while others sat staring vacantly.

As for myself, I was immensely relieved to have escaped from the torture chamber that was my soul. I was thoroughly exhausted and drenched in sweat. And I was still purging. My God! Would I never stop? This was not the time for me to talk. I needed some time to process what had happened. The air outside the Maloca was relatively cool and the stars were amazing! I spent the rest of the night contemplating the ceremony and purging. Just when I thought I had worked through my ordeal, another buried memory would emerge to haunt me. It was near sunrise when I finally stopped having the urge to throw up and I made my way to my mosquito-netted bed and collapsed in exhaustion.

~•~

A troop of monkeys crashing through the trees prodded me out of my deep sleep. I felt emotionally drained and weakened from a night of purging. It was late morning and after a quick bite the group began gathering in the Maloca. It was customary for the group to get together with each other and the shaman and discuss the previous night's ceremony. The conversation was held in English, as again, though we were from all different parts of the globe, it was a common language to everyone except the shaman.

We took turns recounting our experiences while Tatyana or one of the others translated for him. He would then reply making suggestions, observations and interpretations. This was an important part of the ritual, as understanding the plant Mother's healing methods was nearly impossible. Her medicine could be ruthless or beautiful. One thing was apparent. Her techniques were unpredictable, unique, and often extreme. It was very important to hear what the others had gone through to help me understand my journey.

Again, I was amazed by the courage of my new friends as some talked honestly and frankly about things that I am not sure I could have. Some described fantastic visions and other worlds. Some talked of meeting lost loved ones. Others had undergone seemingly nonsensical and fantastical escapades. And for some, like me, the whole thing seemed like a rather wicked nightmare.

When it came my turn, I asked if anyone else had been affected by the moaning and crying that went on thru out the evening. Did anyone else feel his pain? I felt like it had an effect on my experience and I wanted to know if any of the others felt the same way. Apparently, I was alone in my distress. When I told the others about my descent into my personal torture chamber, I was assured that I am not the only one who had been forced to see and deal with past traumas. While I had been aware that this was a possibility, I hadn't thought that I had a lot of things hidden in that deep vault. Boy was I wrong!

The shaman simply said that I had come here to heal, right? Often the way to healing is not pleasant. I had told myself that I had come here for healing from my physical problems. Now, I was not so sure about my motives. It was obvious that Mother Ayahuasca had different ideas about my healing than I did. A door was opening for me. I was beginning to see my health in a whole other light. It was dawning on me that there are many facets to our health. Our physical, mental and emotional health was all intertwined. What affected one aspect affected all aspects. The extent of my irresponsibility was beginning to sink in. I had spent my life living the motto, "live fast and die young." My youth had been spent trying to destroy my body and now I was trying to resurrect it. My eyes were finally being opened to some of the things that I had spent my life ignoring and I was realizing that I wanted to see more!

~•~

After our discussion we were free until the evening ceremony. Some used the time to journal and others to reflect and meditate. I joined a group that was going to visit Monkey Island. I wanted to experience as much of this otherworldly place as I could. We boarded a launch and took off down the mighty river. Flanked by curious porpoises, we meandered downstream through the humidity and blaring sun. I could not imagine this trek in the heat of the summer! We docked in a cove on an island and were promptly boarded by a variety of monkeys of different shapes and sizes. These simians were master thieves and, before I knew it, I had been relieved of my gum in my pocket and the boat was quickly stripped of anything that was not tied down. The monkeys were amazing and cute and a bit scary. After plundering the boat they lost interest in us and went off in search of other mischief.

On the way back to the resort we stopped and swam in a less muddy tributary. The water felt incredible, but I could not put all the creatures I had seen in the river out of my mind. I was so parched that I seemed to absorb the moisture. As soon as I was refreshed I climbed back into the safety of the boat.

~•~

The Maloca was nearly empty when I entered it that evening. I sat next to a nice young man from Canada and we fell into a discussion about the previous ceremony. He had come to meet the Mother after years of depression and a failed suicide attempt. He recounted some particularly bizarre and painful memories that had been brought to light last night. He said he had completely repressed them and had no recollection of them until being forced to relive them in the ceremony. I lent a sympathetic ear as he seemed to need to talk this through. He had been traumatized at a young age and had buried the trauma in a deep place where it could not hurt him. Unfortunately for us, these things we hide can sometimes become infected and start to affect our daily lives. Not only had this painful memory been excavated, he had been shown all the ramifications it had caused in his life. He was still trying to sort it all out and I thought that it was going to be a long process. I could only imagine how repressing such a thing would cause anxiety and depression! At least he had a starting point now, an explanation for the invisible things that had been tormenting him his whole life. He said he was going to sit out tonight's ceremony as he had all he could mentally handle at this point. I told him how much I admired his strength and that I understood his caution and I would be glad to help if he needed to talk.

The others were coming in and getting ready. Shaman Wiler fired up his eternal Mapacho and began summoning us. The ritual had begun. After receiving my potion of mind-bending elixir, I settled back onto my mat and mentally fastened my seatbelt.

~•~

The light was fading rapidly, and I quickly felt the urge to make use of my bucket. The shaman began his powerful Icaros. My eyelids relented as a huge weight settled on them. The moaning and crying began again. Oh no! I was pretty sure that I would not be able to handle another night of his pain! I began to fall in the darkness. Shit! I had a bad feeling about where this was headed. Sure enough, my fall ended in the black hall of reflection!

I was back in Little League. I was laughing at a friend of mine. He was the smart kid in school, but not much of an athlete. Nevertheless, he had joined the team in an effort to fit in with the other kids. He had been at the plate in a stressful point in the game when his bladder gave out. He sank to his knees and the coach made him finish the at bat with urine running down his legs. The pitcher was laughing so hard he could not throw a strike, so my friend earned a base-on-balls. The coach relented and sent me to replace my friend at first base, so he could go clean himself up. The look of hurt and embarrassment on his face when I laughed at him seared my heart. And instantly, I was aware of how this betrayal went on to influence his life. He never played another game of sports in his life and retreated into his books where it was not so painful. He questioned his sexuality and never had any close friends.

I had been oblivious to his pain and my act of indifference would be a wound to my subconscious to which I was also oblivious. And this little memory was not one of the worst! By the end of this night I would be acutely aware that each and every one of these little scars added up to a wound that would stunt my spiritual growth. I could see how these things could ferment and make you ill and prevent you from becoming the person that you could be. I took another tentative step down the endless hall. Staring back at me in the reflection of the black mirror was a memory of myself lying to my father and blaming something on one of my siblings. The causes and effects of this untruth stood out glaringly to me. Another little nick to my soul. My God, would this never end?

I stumbled down this endless dark corridor going from one disappointment to the next. This place was like quicksand for the soul! I would surely become lost here!

Then a gentle touch. A murmur. With great effort I pulled myself from the sludge that was my soul and began to ascend again. I was back in the Maloca and being led to the shaman for his blessing and my Icaro. I remember thinking that he had called me just in time. I could have been lost in that dark place!

His song was powerful, but I was drawn to the soft melodious calling of his wife's birdsong. While kneeling in front of them, I was awed be the simple beauty of their words. Though I could not understand them, the words still held meaning for me. Their voices were the most beautiful and haunting instruments I had ever heard, and I was crestfallen when he anointed me with tobacco smoke and cheap cologne and sent me back to my mat.

As I settled back onto my mat, I was aware again of the moaning and crying that had been a backdrop to the ceremonies up to this point. The shaman and his wife were Mapacho machines and the Maloca was filled with smoke. I was determined not to go back to my little black box of horrors and instead tried to take in what was going on around me in the dark. Try as I might, I could not ignore the painful whimpering that my friend was making. It was like a blanket that, along with the Mapacho smoke, was attempting to suffocate me. I forced myself to stand up. It was as if I was using someone else's body as I staggered to the door. I burst through and gulped down the cool fresh air. The stars in the Amazon are unbelievable, even when you are not in the throes of a powerful hallucinogenic, and the Milky Way was an almost tangible fog across the sky! I was spellbound and immobile and sunk to the wooden decking.

It was probably not long before my rapture was broken by one of the women. She was telling me that I needed to come back inside. I told her that the smoke and the moaning were smothering me and that I need some time. She faded away and I was again beguiled by the immensity of the sky! It could have been hours or minutes before I was stirred from my reverie by a touch. It was Tatyana and she was telling me that I needed to return to the Maloca as the shamans could not protect me out here. She said the jungle was home to many powerful entities and not all of them were benign. I did not feel particularly vulnerable, but I trusted Tatyana and allowed her to guide me back inside.

The rest of the ceremony went quickly. I sat in the darkness and tried to get a sense of how my cohorts were faring. The air of the Maloca was thick with ritual and electric in the way that one could tell powerful forces were at work. When the shamans would begin one of their Icaros, I would lose my tenuous hold on the Maloca and be carried away to some fantastical place beyond imagination and my meager attempts at description. Most of these places were completely foreign to me, totally unfamiliar and incredible to the senses! They were so real in their strangeness, so complete and infinite in detail, that I came to the conclusion that they must be parallel dimensions. I cannot fathom that my mind could create these implausible places in such detail. The Icaros were like a vehicle to transcend space and time! Some places were wonderful and resplendent, and others were gloomy, dangerous and foreboding. Almost all were filled with extraordinary and fantastic life forms.

In between the Icaros, the Maloca would come back into focus and I would try to soak in the experience of the ritual. The others were either in apparent slumber or beginning to stir about, and one was still moaning. After the last of the Icaros, Tatyana began lighting candles marking the end of the ceremony. Soft conversations sprung up and the facilitators began to make the rounds and check on everyone.

I excused myself and, wielding my bucket, I went out on the deck to ponder the stars. It seemed like I was having more of a problem with the purging than the others. I settled in for a long night of star-gazing, trying to identify mysterious jungle sounds and making periodic contributions to my insatiable bucket. I started working through the scars on my soul that the Mother had so unforgivingly pointed out to me. This was not going to be a simple process.

~•~

There would be no ceremony the next evening, so we had a break. I was sure that we all had plenty to think about. We had a morning meeting to share our experiences and concerns about the previous evening's ritual and I was again surprised by my companions' honesty and strength. Some were faring better than others, and some felt the need to share more than others. I didn't really have all that much to talk about. The purging was taking its toll on me and although I was trying to keep hydrated, I had a nagging headache.

A group of us went fishing and I caught one of the most colorful catfish you could imagine on a stick with string. The sun was intense, so we didn't last long.

I grabbed a bag of candy that I had brought with me and I took the short walk along the river bank to the village which was also built on poles. I was drawn to these people that lived out here in this hostile place but went about their business with smiles and laughter.

The village was built around a large open space for all the activities. There were some 20 or so houses on stilts with thatched roofs and no windows. Everyone seemed to know their job, and no one was lounging about even though this was the heat of the day. I sat on a log and watched, trying to fathom their way of life. With no power, running water, church or hospital, these people led an isolated and primitive life. I tried to imagine a life with no television, computers or cell phones. Despite having none of the things that we would call "necessities," they seemed to be able to entertain themselves just fine. I was reminded of my youth, before the advent of cell phones and personal computers, and the things we did to pass the time. To me it seemed like cell phones were meant to make it easier to communicate with each other, but in the end had the opposite effect. We were losing the personal interaction and becoming more distant from each other. These people reminded me of a time when people were more close-knit. I was moved by the intimacy of their families and the community. Their relationships seemed fuller, their lives richer. My society seemed to be racing in the opposite direction. I was deeply troubled by this.

An old woman came and sat next to me. She smiled, and we chatted as she worked on some kind of a reed weaving. She was good natured and had a beatific smile that suggested that she had never met a dentist. The sparkle in her eyes spoke of a healthy love for life and a quick wit. I wondered what vast knowledge of life and nature was stored in their depths. We talked amiably until I made a comment that displayed my typical American arrogance and ignorance. I asked her if there was anything that they needed, anything I could do to help.

She gave me a scornful look and replied, "Why do you think we need your help? Do we look that poor and unhappy? We have everything we need here. The river gives us food and water for our fields. The trees give us fruit. What do you think you could give us? Oh, I know." She had a mischievous glint in her eyes now. She had spotted the bag of candy in my hands.

When I left she was handing out Jolly Ranchers to a group of chattering young children who had materialized out of thin air. I walked back to the camp more than a bit chagrined, thinking that I had a lot to learn about necessity and happiness. Later, we would return as a group when the women had all their wares on display. It was an amazing array of items, all harvested from the natural materials of the jungle. Most were destined for the tourist market in Beline, but this was a chance for them to sell their goods without a middle man. I bought a bunch of stuff that I could give as gifts when I got home. I was glad that I hadn't spent my money in the tourist traps in Iquitos. This was another way that the retreat aided these hardworking people. They brought the tourists directly to this remote place and the villagers did not have to haul their bounty to market.

Some of us had brought things like crayons and coloring books, tee shirts and candy as gifts in appreciation for taking care of us out here in this timeless place where we would surely parish without them. The children were impossibly cute when they saw the gifts and their eyes lit up. I had a vision of those same children with cell phones in their hands and I felt an intense sorrow that these people's delicate and fascinating way of life was speeding to an unwanted end. Instead of pity I was envious of their closeness to nature and to each other. I thought that if I could truly give them a gift it would be to somehow shield them from the inevitable onslaught of technology that was marching towards them.

~•~

Back at the compound I had the chance to talk with one of the facilitators about my first two ceremonies. My purging seemed obsessive and I was doing my best to keep hydrated, but I had to force myself to eat. I was concerned about being trapped in the black box of my memories and asked her if this was all I had to look forward to in the next ceremony?

She suggested that I try to use a mantra. She said it helped her escape from those places where she didn't want to go. It also helped make our intentions known to the Mother. She also explained that the young man who had been moaning and crying had decided that he was not going to participate in the next ceremony. He had come as support to a friend and he was only partaking of the Ayahuasca to support her. Amazingly he could remember nothing of the two previous night's rituals, and felt he was not getting anything out of ordeals. His friend, on the other hand, had experienced two incredible sessions and believed she had already worked out the issues the she had come to address.

This was a huge relief to me! I had considered not participating because I did not think I could handle another night of his pain. She explained that his plight could be what happened when someone did not believe and was not open to the medicine. The Mother was a fickle healer and she would not abide insincerity. He would get nothing from her but pain. Unfortunately for me, I had a strong sense of empathy and was not benefitting from his conflict. She also suspected that I was trying to control my interaction with the medicine. Up until this point I had not been aware of trying to control my episodes. I saw that in trying to escape going to that black box of my soul that I was indeed trying to control my visions. I should try to use my mantra to show my intent and try not to disrespect the Mother by attempting to force my will.

~•~

When I walked into the Maloca for the third ceremony I was determined to leave my ego outside. I came early and sat quietly trying to clear my mind of my fears and expectations. I wanted to demonstrate my blossoming respect for the Mother's powers and my willingness to submit to her ministrations. I thought I would keep my mantra simple: "I am yours, I seek healing, please be gentle with me." I would invoke it when I started to feel distraught or in danger or simply to state my intentions.

After drinking the sacred, but foul-tasting medicine, I lay on my mat and recited my mantra until the purging began and the light faded away. Shaman Wiler's Icaros were especially moving! Their words became colors and smells and I would have the sensation of traveling great distances until the tapestry of light and sounds solidified into some impossible alien landscape. The terrain, the creatures and plant life in these exotic lands are well beyond my ability to relate. Suffice it to say that nothing in my lifetime had prepared me for this journey into the unfamiliar. The vividness and resplendent colors and textures of these other dimensions were beyond psychedelic! The shaman's voice would drive me to these improbable places, but it was his wife Angela's voice that beckoned to me. Her song transformed into a fairy-like light entity that would lead me through these extraterrestrial neighborhoods. Some of these places were stunning beyond words in their splendor while others were dark and filled with vicious looking creatures of mal intent! In these cases, I would recite my mantra and look for my fairy guide and I would follow her into the ether where the kaleidoscope of colors would eventually reform into another world beyond my comprehension.

The Mother had obviously decided that I had been punished enough and I had no idea why she was showing me otherworldly places other than to show me that my reality was not the only one. The overall experience of this ceremony was like going on an incredible documentary of the universe. It left me feeling that I knew nothing and that all my previous knowledge was baseless and useless. The universe was vast and unimaginable, and I was looking at it thru a pinhole! The immensity of all that I did not know was staggering and I could not fathom it in a million lifetimes!

When I left the Maloca that night I was confused and disappointed. Although this night's ceremony had not been a painful nightmare, I was still purging. Most of the others did not have this problem. Was I purging to release more toxins from my body? I was beginning to suspect that the purging, lack of sleep and being able to eat very little was starting to become a problem. I spent another night on the deck, throwing up and staring into the endless sea of stars. We had one more ceremony the next night and then we would be heading home. I was no closer to figuring out why I had been called here or what, if anything, I was getting out of it.

~•~

I was a late riser the next morning and the meeting was already underway when I entered the Maloca. A blinding headache and a weak stomach made me feel like I was walking aboard a ship. When it came to be my turn I told the others that I didn't think I would attend the last ceremony. I told them that I was not sure I would survive another night of purging. I did not think I was getting anything out of this ordeal that would make another night of throwing up worth it. Shaman Wiler and Tatyana did not look pleased. She translated for him that no one had ever died from the sacred plant medicine and it would be a shame to back out now. I had come a long way at considerable expense; did I not want to see this through? Although I knew I was not one to walk away, I could not imagine going through another ceremony feeling as sick as I did. I told them I would try to hydrate and see if I felt better.

Shaman Wiler poured cold water over my head and sang a chant as he massaged my temples. He made me a batch of tea and the veil that was blinding me slowly dissipated. I spent the afternoon drinking water and thinking about my dilemma. The plant Mother's healing methods made no sense to me, but I was beginning to have a deep respect for her powers. She had been doing this for thousands of years and I was starting to discover just how little that I knew about life. Who was I to question her methods? Here I was trying to analyze and control things again. I decided that I was on a trip of discovery and that I would not succumb to my fear and ignorance. I would put my trust in the Mother's compassion and wisdom. My intuition was that she knew what was best for me even though I could not understand her ways. Maybe it was my destiny to die out here in the middle of nowhere. Or could this be the center of the universe? At least I would die seeking knowledge and a better way to live this life!

~•~

When I entered the temple that evening I was greeted with words of encouragement by these kind people that cared about me enough to worry. Shaman Wiler had told me that while he would perform his duty to the others, he was going to concentrate on helping me this evening. He didn't ask how much of the elixir I wanted this time and just handed me the cup. Surprisingly the drink didn't offend me as much this time. When I settled back onto my mat I did not feel the need to purge myself of the medicine at all. The opposite was actually true. I felt a sort of euphoria.

The Icaros started and I was summoned to the shamans. Their song was impossibly haunting and moving. I was so affected by the chant that it took some gentle prodding to get me to return to my mat. At the start of the next Icaro I was swept away into the ether only to find myself in what had to be the mythical Garden of Eden having an intense conversation with a huge serpent about truth. His argument was very persuasive! He was suggesting that most everyone went about their lives doing, saying things to impress those around us and never daring to speak the truth. We all just follow along, not wanting to be the one who causes a ripple. Always afraid to do or say anything that would draw the scrutiny of our peers. That most of us are not true to ourselves and that we spend our lives conforming.

Our rather one-sided debate was interrupted when what appeared to be an angel grabbed my hand and led me back to the shamans for another Icaro. After another ballad that seemed to intensify the amount of energy in the Maloca, Shaman Wiler anointed me with more tobacco smoke and cheap cologne and sent me back to my mat.

Before I knew it, I was in some sort of alien jungle. The unfamiliar vegetation was thick and there was a palpable tension here. My instincts told me I was in danger and I began to scan the foliage for threats. With all things being unfamiliar it was particularly hard to discern the threats. The hair on my arms stood up as I was able to distinguish four tall humanoid shapes hiding in the shadows. They all seemed to have the same evil looking wooden masks and sported spears. I was terrified and started to flee. The jungle was too dense and I could not make much headway. The ghostly apparitions were easily able to maintain pace on their long legs. I ran for what seemed like forever when one of the creatures seemed to tire of the game. In a deft move he came at me and ran me through with his spear and lifted me high in the air! I remember thinking that the damn shaman had told me no one dies from ceremony! I began to recite my mantra as he waved me in the air.

A cool touch and the call of my name distracted me. Another angel was calling me, urging me to come back to the shaman for another Icaro. I was swimming through the ether until the myriad of colors began to solidify and the Maloca began to coalesce around me. It felt like home and not a moment too soon! I checked myself for holes and went to kneel in front of the shaman. He met my accusatory stare with a grin and sang me a mind-blowing song. He then blew Mapacho on me, blessed me, spit some cologne on me and sent me back to my mat again. I remember thinking that I would not be smelling good after this was over. They should save the floral bath for after!

This time when the singing started I was not transported to some unimaginable place but stayed rooted to my mat. I was transfixed by the sight of an incredible light-being that was crossing the Maloca towards me. It had a vaguely human shape that seemed familiar to me. The being stopped in front of me and began to sing a song that worked in harmony with the shamans'. I could not make out the language, but the singer's voice was evocative and ethereal and somehow recognizable. The being started to undulate in time to the music. Slowly, the dance intensified, and the figure began to transform. The light that this entity was emitting was dimming and it was changing shape. Soon it had gone from a beacon of light to a dark shape that was blacker than the lightless Maloca. As the dance continued the black form took the shape of a great black condor. I was mesmerized by the song and the dance of the terrible visage and had the feeling it was trying to tell me something, but I was unable to understand. The dance and song faded, but the apparition remained standing before me with its wings spread wide.

The mighty condor was intimidating but seemed to be offering an invitation. I stood and went to the magnificent bird and was enveloped by its wings. A sensation of pure love washed over me, and I realized that it was speaking to me in a language that I could understand. It was a kind a gentle female voice that I recognized from somewhere.

She told me that I had done the right thing in coming here. She said that the great Mother Ayahuasca worked in mysterious ways and that I was getting the healing that I needed even if it did not feel like it. In time I would begin to understand more. She said that I had been called here and that this was all part of a bigger picture. Whether I knew it or not, I was now in the employ of the forces that had summoned me here. She said that I was a natural leader and that others would follow me. She told me that I had work to do, that there was a movement coming and I that was needed to help spread the word. When she released me, I could feel the light of that pure love shining inside me and I hoped that it was a lasting gift.

The Dream

I returned to the mat with my head and my heart reeling. The great bird had vanished, but I still felt its glow within me. Before I could make sense of its words, I felt a light touch and I was being called to the shamans for another Icaro. I was still filled with the gift of the Condor and this Icaro brought the intensity of the ceremony to new heights. I seemed to float back to my mat and I felt everything was vibrating at a higher frequency. I closed my eyes and was instantly traveling through the cosmos.

When I came to rest I was in the most beautiful place one could imagine. I was in a meadow of flowers of every hue surrounded by a dense jungle. The colors, sounds and smells almost overloaded the senses. Every flower pedal, every leaf and vine were impossibly magnificent! Outrageously colored birds called out bewitching lullabies. Extravagant butterfly-like creatures flitted through the plants chased by fairies. The smells were bizarre and exotic and there was a cacophony of creature calls that sounded like a symphony. Peering through the foliage were outlandish beasts and freakish looking fauna.

As I looked about in abject wonder, something detached itself from the tree canopy and started floating down into the glade. I gasped in astonishment as I realized that this fabulous being was a kind of plant-human chimera. That she was female was beyond question as her body had unmistakable curves. She glided down to the clearing on wings of great green leaves veined with rainbows. She wore a cloak of many colored cloves and in her fabulous hair of creepers was a crown of flowers. Her bark-like skin made her look ancient, but her countenance screamed youthful vitality. She came to rest in front of me and I was instantly paralyzed by her most arresting feature.

Dios mio! Her eyes!

They were at once childlike and ancient! They brimmed with compassion and were as cold as ice! Bright with inquisitiveness and deep as the ocean! They held the promise of all that is, was and ever will be! How easy it would be to lose oneself in their depths! The truths and knowledge that might be found there! I knew instinctively that in going there I would be forever lost. There would be no return! This was undoubtedly the entity who had spent the last 5 days tormenting me.

It was she! I had been granted audience with the Mother Ayahuasca! She was ancient yet beautiful beyond words or comprehension! Here was a being that transcended time and dimensions and she was smiling at me as if I was her favorite child!

I had traveled thousands of miles and spent countless hours trying to ready myself mentally for this possibility! No amount of written or spoken word could prepare me for this encounter and I knew that my whole life had been leading up to this moment.

My reverie was broken when I realized that she was speaking. I did not hear these words as much as they seemed to materialize as concepts in my head. Her words transcended any language, it was pure thought. She was inside my head and I would be hiding nothing from her.

Her demand was clear to me. She wished to know what had brought me here.

I formed the answer that she surely already knew ... I told her I had come to be healed.

"I understand that is what you believe that you need," she replied in a voice that was laced with the wisdom of eons. She smiled kindly and said, "Very well then."

She lifted into the air and began a dance that would make a fairy blush. As she flitted about she left trails of bewitching rainbows. The intricate gyrations of her dance would start slowly and build to a crescendo. She would pause in mid-air and with a beat of her great leaf-wings a wave of energy would wash over me. As it passed over and through me I could see a black toxic substance falling away from me. With each beat of her mighty wings more and more of the noxious sludge detached and fell away from me. She continued until the well of toxins within me was washed clean. When she stopped I felt as clean and transparent as a wraith. She performed an elaborate curtsy and when she settled back to earth words began to form in my head.

"You asked to be healed and I have rid you of all that is holding you back, child. Go now and I ask only one thing in return. In your travels others will come to you. You must pass on the knowledge of the Mother that you have received today. Great change is coming, and I am here to help. If you need me; now you know how to find me."

With that, her world started to fade until all that was left were those incredible eyes! I was moving through the ether again and the Maloca soon began to take shape around me. I sat there on my mat in stunned silence. The ceremony was over and candles were being lit and I sat there, unable to move. All that I had experienced that night was replaying in my head. Conversations with gigantic intellectual reptilians. My death at the hands of mask wearing monsters. The incredible Condor dance by the light being! And to top it off, the meeting with the entity which could only be the plant Mother in the meadow!

Someone asked me how my ceremony went, and I stood up and stretched and said that it had been incredible, and I felt amazing. The whole Maloca erupted in applause and I realized that I had been helped by everyone there as they had all been pulling for me. This night I was full of energy and eager to talk to my friends about the night's events.

There was one thing I needed to know first. I sought out Tatyana and asked her if she had made a visit to my mat at any point in the ceremony? She smiled shyly and said that she had. I said that it had been one of the most beautiful things I had ever seen! I was disappointed to find out that I was the only one that had witnessed it. I asked her what had prompted her to do that. She told me that occasionally during ceremony she would be possessed by a higher power and would act as a conduit. She said she really didn't remember the dance or what had been said. I tried unsuccessfully to tell her how beautiful it had been and how much it meant to me. I wondered if she knew just how powerful she was.

I would spend hours with my friends talking about the ceremony, about how this journey had affected us and where we would go from here. We all felt that we had been changed at a basic level by our experiences and now it was up to us to find out just how much. When you have been through an intense ordeal such as we had it forms an enduring bond. Although I knew that we would all be going out separate ways, I was reluctant for our adventure to come to an end. I would miss these courageous young explorers! This was our last night together. Tomorrow we would go back to Iquitos and from there we would go home. I had a strange feeling that home would never be the same place to me again.

~•~

In the morning we all met to go over the ceremony, say our goodbyes and exchange info with the inevitable promise to keep in touch. It was an amazing and powerful thing we had done. We came from all corners of the planet, strangers, to meet in the jungle, bare our souls to each other, find the healing we were seeking, and then return to our lives. In a short time, we had forged strong bonds, similar I think to survivors of a tragedy.

After many pictures and promises we hauled our stuff to the dock and boarded the peche peches for a long trip back to Iquitos. I felt a strange reluctance to leave this primitive land that was so steeped in mystery and ancient wisdom. I felt that it had given me so much! There was plenty of time to reflect on my experiences on the way back.

That we had been changed was a given. In the following months it would become apparent just how changed we were. I think one of the gifts or consequences of working with the plant Mother is that she strips away the veil of untruth that seems to keep us from seeing the world as it really is. Most of us would realize that we had been living meaningless lives trying to impress people that really don't matter. We work our butts off to scrape out a living while making others rich. We would see the futility of such a life. There are very few rewards in a life of servitude. And the sad part is we never really know who it is we are serving or why. All the tools that the rich use to keep us ignorant and in fear stand out glaringly. After working with the Mother, it is hard to find meaning in such a life. It can leave a person with little tolerance for the American ideal and those who follow blindly along. Even though we know that they are good people who just can never stop and look around them. To this day I prefer not to suffer fools and that can make a person lonely.

~•~

As you might imagine, seeing things in a whole new light can make returning to a meaningless life very difficult. One of our group returned and lost his business because he couldn't bare the hustle and was no longer driven by the greed that pervades life in the United States. I can only hope that he found a way to make his way that didn't compromise his morals and gave him some happiness. The importance of doing what you love and loving what you do was never so glaring to me.

Another tough aspect of trying to re-integrate into a life that now seemed foreign to us was the fact that it is extremely hard to find anyone else that you can confide in. No one knows the things you have learned, seen, and done and they cannot relate. Like it or not, most people were going to look at us in a different light, most would think we were crazy. Some of us were bound to walk a lonely path in life unless we could find others who looked at the world in similar ways.

The other side to the coin is that Ayahuasca opens us up to our inner creativity. Some of us would leave our meaningless jobs and find others where we could be creative and fulfilled. In the long run, we may not be "successful" in the ways of Capitalism, but our success would be rooted in being and doing what makes us happy. I was one of the lucky ones as I had no disappointing job to return to and I didn't give a hoot what people thought of me.

That the Mother had cleansed me of harmful memories and traumas was becoming more apparent. I had never felt so light of spirit! As painful as it had been, it was like being freed of invisible life-long bonds that were holding me back from being who I could be. I was now happy with myself. I don't know if I knew what real happiness was before. I had based it on all the wrong things.

The Mother had also opened up a whole new universe of possibilities. I now knew that there were so many things all around us to which we are blind. I had met a benevolent entity that was as real as you and I and she wanted to help us. Her conditions might be a bit harsh, but her gifts were worth the cost. I had shed the veil that they used to keep us blind and afraid. I had faced my fears and my life was now full of wonders. I was eager to explore and seek knowledge with these new eyes in places that I had not known existed before. I felt that my past was a previous life, to be learned from but not relived. I was looking forward to a life of living each day to the fullest. I was like a child, everything being new to me again. I could not wait for tomorrow just to see what marvels it might bring.

As we motored down the gigantic river back towards the lives that now seemed so foreign to us, I reflected on my choice to follow my dream. My journey had taken me to a land of dreams. Peru will always be a country of mysteries, of secrets and of untold possibilities to me. I am eternally grateful for her gifts to me. I am not sure that I got what I went there for, but I am positive that I got much more than I paid for.

Chapter Six
Mexico

Apparently, the Mother had gifted me with the glow that I had first noticed with the group of young explorers that were returning from the jungle in Cusco. For several months after my return, people that I knew, and some I did not, would approach me and ask what was happening with me. Some said my aura stood out. Others simply said that I was glowing. An overwhelming peacefulness had enveloped me. I was very aware of all that was happening around me. The negative things like politics, greed and all the injustices which litter our lives glared at me. On the other hand, I was seeing beauty in places where I had never ventured to look. And the beauty and wonders of the world were winning out over the many negatives. For once I was able to turn my back on those things that would previously have clung to me, weighing me down. When asked, I would fulfill my promise and relate my journey to Peru and my life changing encounter with the Mother. Most had never heard of Ayahuasca and fewer could relate to my journey, but nearly all would say that I had unique air about me.

For my part, since my cleansing from the Mother, I had never felt so light of soul. It seemed I was free of the shackles of my demons and I had never felt so unencumbered. For the first time in my life I felt completely at peace with myself. I felt no need to act in a certain way to impress others. Try as I might, I could no longer find that part of me that was concerned with what others thought. My ego had diminished. My previous goals of "success" were irrelevant. I felt free and light and happy! I realized that I had lived a long life without ever knowing real happiness. I looked back at my former self and felt nothing but pity and sorrow. I vowed that I would devote my life to the pursuit of those things that made me happy. I had the belief that if I could reach that state of contentment and harmony with Mother Nature, then all good things would come.

Unfortunately for me, I could find very few people with whom I could relate. Everyone I knew was caught up in the rat race that is modern day life. Politics, debt, greed, the never-ending battle to make ends meet, all these things combine to keep us from the really important thing in life. To be happy! I looked around at all those good people walking dazedly through the grind of everyday life and they all seemed tired, worn-out and frustrated. I could not find one person that was truly happy with their life. I longed for the simple and pure life that I had seen in Peru. It seemed to me that those people who had nothing, also seemed to have everything that we in the States had lost. Their lives were richer. Their struggles were more basic and real. Their loves more passionate.

Within a month of returning, I had realized that Bisbee was no longer my home. I was not going to fall back into the apathy that had ruled my life. Since my operation I had received permanent disability. The amount of my check allowed me to live a meager life of just getting by. I could see that in time I would begin to accrue debt and would eventually be enslaved again by the monetary machine.

A plan began to take shape. My money would go way further in a country like Mexico or further south. I felt no need for material things; in fact, I had an overwhelming urge to rid myself of the things that were tying me down. I made the decision to sell my house and all my belongings. I would travel south and look for a place where I could begin anew in a simple life. Perhaps I could find a place where I could contribute to a good cause, teach kids or sustainability. I had loads of construction and architectural experience. I had knowledge and experience to share. I had things I could give. Surely, I could find a place where I could help in some way and lead a more fulfilling way of life.

With my mind made up, I made the phone call to the realtor and went about telling my astonished family and friends. I was initially met with concern and disbelief. The concept of ridding myself of all my possessions and embarking on a solo journey into unknown territory was beyond most people. Wasn't I afraid? Everyone had heard of the dangers of those third world countries. Had I lost my mind?

I have always had a restless soul and a need to explore. I blame my yearning for adventure on my parents. For some reason beyond my understanding, my parents had felt the need to have ten children. My father had been an officer in the army and had traveled extensively in his tour of duty. Growing up, we were lucky to stay in one place for more than a couple years. As a result, we were constantly moving to different schools and leaving our old friends behind. The positive thing about this was we learned how to make new friendships and how to adapt to new situations.

In the late sixties my parents were dismayed by the drug culture that was prevalent in Northern California at the time. When I was twelve years old my father retired, sold his house, packed his remaining six children at home into the van and moved to Mexico. We spent two years there in a noble, but failed attempt to shield his children from the influence of drugs.

This was a very trying time for me. My parents were taking me away from my friends and my passion, sports. I would hold this against my parents for some time to come. In the long run, however, I would come to realize that the things I learned in Mexico would benefit me more than being able to play sports.

My father was an amazing man. He had the rare ability to treat everyone with the same respect that he commanded. There were no ups and downs with him. He was a rock. He was unthreatening and therefore was not threatened. In this way he was able to handle almost any situation that confronted him. He had a way of breezing through life on the wings of common decency. This was his greatest lesson to me, and I would live my life without fear, confident in my abilities to make my way through almost any situation.

My mother was amazing in her own right. She was a devoted wife and mother and followed her man wherever he went, supporting him in whatever he did. Raising ten very independent children, often by herself, and traveling endlessly took another sort of power. She was of that generation that never complained but just got things done. Although she stood by her man, she had a will of her own and came equipped with a quick wit. They never forced their ideologies on us and encouraged free-thinking. This ended up making their lives difficult as it resulted in having to raise ten very strong-willed, independent and often trouble-prone children. There was always plenty of food in our house and usually one or two of their children's friends hanging about.

In my two years in Mexico I would become fluent in Spanish and fall in love with the Mexican people and their zest for life. I would become enamored with adventure and history. I would eventually forgive my parents for denying me the sports that I loved. The many lessons learned in living in a foreign country would far outweigh the benefits of growing up in a sheltered California lifestyle.

So, no, I wasn't afraid. I loved the Mexican people and their laid-back way of life. I knew enough of the world to avoid most bad situations. I was confident in myself, with humanity, and with my abilities.

My friends and family were not thrilled with my decision. This journey of mine was beyond their comprehension. They knew I had been through a lot in the last few years and they thought I would be much safer close to home and near the doctors. In the end, they would all give me their blessings because all they wanted for me was to be happy. They knew that I am happiest when exploring, meeting people and living life! I had no idea how much more time I had allotted to me, but I was not going to sit back and wait to die. There were too many mysteries and wonders in this world and I was just beginning to open my eyes.

~•~

After my surgery and during the time when the doctors were trying to remove the stone from my pancreas, I would occasionally visit my sister who was living in San Carlos, Mexico at the time. San Carlos is a sleepy Anglo enclave on the Sea of Cortez, an easy six-hour drive south of Bisbee. A good portion of my life had been spent on the coast of California and in Arizona. As a result, the beach and the desert were where I felt most at home. San Carlos appealed to me because it had both - desert right up to the beach.

During my visits I would stay at the trailer park where my sister was living. It was a small, intimate trailer park run by a Canadian expat and his Mexican wife. It was while staying here that I met my friend Chapo. As a result of his good nature, the owner of the park was forever rescuing stray dogs, of which there seemed to be an endless supply. Chapo and his sister Mia were benefactors of his kindness, as he had rescued them from the streets and had taken a liking to them.

Chapo was not your ordinary street dog. Most of these dogs, because of their hard lives were straggly and people wary. Chapo, on the other-hand, was outgoing and unusually intelligent. He seemed to be somewhat of a prince of street dogs and he has a rather regal trot and bearing that sets him apart from other dogs. We hit it off instantly and Chapo followed me around when I was there. I would take him and his sister and the other dogs living in the park for long walks for my exercise. I actually asked his owner if I could have him several times. Although Chapo was supposed to be a guard dog for the trailer park he was too amiable and did not bark. Nonetheless, everyone in the park loved Chapo and he was not about to let Chapo go.

I made several trips to San Carlos and each time it was harder to leave Chapo. He would follow my truck when I left, and it broke my heart. On my last visit Chapo followed me all the way to town and even started to follow me down the highway. When I brought him back to the trailer park I made one last plea to the owner to let Chapo come home with me.

"No," he told me. "You can't take my dog."

As I was saying goodbye to my friend, the owner's wife came out and stood watching us. It was obvious who was the real boss here when she turned to her husband and said, "What's the matter with you? Can't you see that Chapo loves him?" She looked at me and said, "Chapo is your dog now."

"You can't just give my dog away!" he cried.

"I can too, and I just did!" she told him.

"You two belong together." She smiled and told me to enjoy him. When her husband started to complain, she stifled him with a withering look and went back in the house. Since that day Chapo is my constant companion and he considers my truck to be his own. He is forever cheerful and has helped me to endure some pretty rough times. When I returned from a month in Peru it took him several days to forgive me for my absence. He finally relented when I told him that I would never leave him again. We have a rare kind of bond. He needs very little instruction from me and we seem to be telepathically linked. He usually does what needs to be done without having to be told. He is simply the best dog on the planet and we have become more than best friends. He is more of a companion than a pet and our respect is mutual. I would not be going to Mexico alone.

~•~

It took me six months to sell my house. In the daytime I would address the myriad of problems involved in selling a 90-year-old house. At night I would research Mexico and the countries of Central America. I had no real destination and planned to keep going until I found my ideal spot. I figured that I would recognize it when I saw it.

My 2003 Toyota Tundra had always been reliable, so I went through it mechanically to make sure it was sound. I purchased a cab-over camper and tried to imagine what I would need to bring with me. I was pretty familiar with Mexico and had a fairly good idea what I would need to bring and what could be purchased there. Beyond Mexico, I had no idea, so I wanted to cover the essentials. Six months is a long time to plan and when I finally hit the road I had everything I would need to camp out and be self-sufficient until my water ran out.

I practiced the things I had learned in Peru. Each day, preferably at sunset, Chapo and I would find ourselves out in the desert, away from humanity, sitting quietly and practicing breathing. I used the memory of sitting with my back to the wall in Machu Picchu and breathing in time with the vibrating earth to calm myself. With much practice, I was able to release the things that bothered me about living in the United States. Not only was I happy, I was beginning to learn how to stay that way. I was able to let things go that would have clung to me and bothered me before. As for Chapo, he would pause his ceaseless foraging for rabbits to sit calmly by my side. I believe Chapo likes to meditate.

~•~

Ever since the dream that called me to Peru, I had been infatuated with dreaming. I felt there was a connection between the otherworldly places I was shown during the Ayahuasca ceremonies and the places we went to in our dreams. I suspected that these places were more real than I had previously given them credit for. In my evenings I began to search for places and people in Mexico that might be able to help me learn more. One evening I found a website for the Centre of the Conscious Dream in San Luis Potosi. The Centre used Toltec teachings and had courses in shamanic training. The teachings were centered around dreaming with intent. In other words, they taught that one could be an active participant in one's dreams. Once a person could control their dreams then it was possible to travel great distances and enter other dimensions. They teach us to relate to the elements of nature, the plants and animals and trees. It also relates the earth, moon, sun and stars and how to find our place of balance.

This seemed like an excellent place to find the answers that were plaguing me. I got in touch with the creator of the Centre and arranged to meet him at his home in San Francisco, in the state of Nayararit. This was a little town about half way down the Pacific Coast of Mexico. I had been planning on going down the Pacific side of Mexico as I was already familiar with it, having spent a year in Manzanillo with my parents. I loved the pristine beaches and planned to take my time and explore every one of them I could get to.

Now I had the makings of a plan. I did not want to make too many more plans and wanted to play my journey by ear, but it felt good to have a first destination. All I need now was someone to buy my house!

By the time someone decided to relieve me of my house, I was itching to start my journey. The last six months had seemed like an eternity! I said my goodbyes to my friends and family. This turned out to be very hard for me. For all I knew, this would be the last time I would see many of them and I loved them dearly. My dilemma was to stay among my loved ones and lead a life that I knew would be disappointing or to follow my heart. I chose to follow the voice that was whispering the call of my destiny.

~•~

Early one spring morning I crossed the border and left my life as I knew it behind. I was at once exhilarated and sorrowful. Choosing to leave my family and friends had been harder than I imagined. I realized as I drove that I had no intention of returning. In one way I felt selfish but another I felt like I was finally doing something real and for myself. I would not be conforming to the brainwashed status quo, I would live life on my own terms and for that, I was proud of myself.

My trip had a rather inauspicious start as I hit Mazatlan at the same time as a large hurricane did. The whole area was flooded, and I was stuck there for several days. Mazatlan is the first major tourist destination along the Pacific coast and is large and bustling with resorts. This was not the type of place I was drawn to and was eager to leave as soon as the roads cleared.

My next stop was San Blas, a sleepy town on the beach off the tourist's radar. While I liked the atmosphere there, I was unprepared for the veracity of the mosquitoes! I checked into a nice motel and Chapo and I eagerly went to explore the beach. I have done many things in my life, but I think my real calling is to be a beach-bum. I could never tire of the beach and Mexico has some of the most breathtaking. This was the rainy season in San Blas and I had heard rumors that the mosquitoes here could be bad. Well, that was a complete understatement! Even armed with a liberal dousing of extra-strength repellent, I was assaulted ruthlessly as Chapo and I made the short walk to the beach. When we got to the beach, the assault began in earnest. I had mosquitoes in my hair, ears and eyes. They were in between my toes and up my shorts. Chapo was faring no better and I was amazed to see him swatting at the pests with his paws. We beat a hasty retreat to our motel, but the damage had already been done.

When I woke up the next morning I was astonished to find that I could not move a muscle without experiencing acute pain! I could literally not get out of bed. I had no idea what was happening to me. I could not even raise my hand to my face. After an eternity, I managed to roll out of bed and had to crawl to the bathroom. I had never experienced anything like this. Every part of my body hurt. I managed to crawl out my front door and was seen by an employee of the motel. He helped me to the front desk and I explained my situation to the matronly woman in charge. She told me that I most likely had the mosquito sickness called "dengue." She could recognize the symptoms because nearly everyone in San Blas had dengue at one time in their lives.

What followed is one of the main reasons I love the Mexican people. The kind woman behind the desk ran this particular motel with her four sisters. She immediately took control and summoned a taxi to take me to the doctor. She said she would watch over Chapo until I got back. To my chagrin, the doctor confirmed her assessment saying that there was nothing to do but let the infection run its course. I asked him how long it would take, and he said anywhere from three days to a week. When the taxi deposited me back at the hotel, the gracious proprietor said not to worry, she and her sisters would take care of me until I was better. With some help from a worker, I made the painful way back to my bed where I would remain for the next four days.

The Dream

The owner and her sisters were true to their word and hovered over me like I was in an exclusive hospital. They would take Chapo for walks several times a day and were constantly trying to get me to eat meals prepared especially for me. After four miserable days the fever lifted and I was eager to leave this haven of blood-thirsty insects. I cannot imagine what would have happened if I had decided to camp out on the beach instead of taking a motel room. I was dreading settling the bill, as I had no clue what all this attention was going to cost. When I went to check out, I was stunned to find out that the angelic sisters would accept no money for the food, the stay or any of their many ministrations. They said it was not my fault that I had taken ill and the only form of payment she would accept was a recommendation on their website. I was moved to tears by their kindness and thought that something like this would never have happened in the States where all is driven be greed and profit lines. I flashed back on a speech by our president calling the Mexican people thieves and drug addicts. These people were beautiful and more hospitable than most people in the States would ever know. I felt extremely grateful to be among them and out of the influence of the ignorance and greed that ruled peoples' lives up north.

By this time Chapo had won over the entire workforce of the hotel and after many pictures and heartfelt thanks, we took our leave of the kindhearted sisters of San Blas and continued down the coast. By this time the desert had turned to lush jungle-like greenery. We were now below the Sea of Cortez and the coast was now exposed to the great Pacific Ocean. San Blas, it seems, was an anomaly where the voracious insect population is concerned, and as we worked our way south the mosquitoes relented their reign. I was in no hurry and would explore each and every road that turned off the highway and looked as if it might cleave through the dense jungle to the coast. Chapo and I were lucky to find a few small fishing villages without restaurants or hotels but where we could camp on the beach. In this way we made our way slowly down the coast. We avoided the cities and sought out the places unknown to tourists. Sometimes we would camp for days, fishing, swimming and doing the almost unbearable work of beach bums. The only people we met were the campesinos and fishermen who worked in these remote places. They were always helpful and inquisitive as to what this gringo and his dog were doing out in the middle of nowhere.

Having lost all sense of time and urgency, Chapo and I were brought back to reality when we rolled into the sleepy beach town of San Francisco. I had almost forgotten that I had promised to meet the creator of the Centre of the Conscious Dream here. I instantly fell in love with San Francisco, which apparently also goes by the alias of San Pancho or even San Felipe. This was a kind of a boutique tourist town that was not well known to your average vacationer. The pastime here was surfing and I was amazed to see the whole town turn out almost every evening to watch the inevitable spectacular sunsets over the water. The town was full of friendly, outgoing young people who have an infectious thirst for life. I was surprised and moved when the whole town burst into spontaneous cheers and applause as the sun made an exceptionally beatific plunge into the endless blue ocean. This was an event I can't even imagine happening in the

States and again I felt fortunate to be here and very at home with these people.

It seemed that Daniel, the teacher who had built the Centre of the Conscious Dream, was a busy man and we had to wait several days for a meeting with him. This was fine with me, as I was in no hurry to leave this magical little enclave. Chapo became somewhat of a celebrity in town and within a few days everyone seemed to know his name. They found it particularly amusing that he bore the same name as "El Chapo," an all-powerful drug lord who basically ruled the region.

Chapo and I were sitting in an outdoor fruit-drink stand waiting to meet Daniel when we were approached by a soft-spoken man with an English accent. I was a bit taken aback when he asked if I was Chris and introduced himself as Daniel. He was dressed in loose fitting cotton and sandals and had an easy-going air about him. Daniel was accompanied by a young man who was obviously the center of his world, and who he introduced as his son, Venato. I had mistakenly assumed that a teacher of Toltec knowledge would be someone of indigenous heritage. I must admit that I was somewhat put off by the thought of being taught the mysteries of Toltec wisdom by an expat Englishman. As he began to talk, I quickly realized that his ancestry had nothing to do with the knowledge that he was offering to share with me. As we talked Daniel seemed to be interviewing me much as I was him. He was very casual and self-assured and seemed to be slightly amused at life. His manner put me completely at ease and I liked him instantly.

Daniel first told me about himself. He had been born in England and lived there through his college days. He found himself at odds with the conventional thinking of his countrymen and decided to travel the world seeking some meaning. His search led him to Tibet and the Middle East where he studied for some time. He then went to South America studying shamanism and the ancient ways. Eventually he ended up in Mexico where the teachings of the Toltec shamans resonated deeply with him. When I met Daniel, he had been living in Mexico for many years. He had been driven to build the Centre of the Conscious Dream by a dream. It was to be built in a magical place in the high desert that was near a sacred site of the Huichol Indians called Wirikuta. He built a small compound there with no running water or electricity where he brought small groups seeking his instruction. This had been a holy place since beyond memory and here technology held no sway.

After telling me about the Centre, he asked me about myself. I told him of my health issues and my trip to Peru to meet the Mother Ayahuasca. He listened politely and then he asked me if I would like to be able to reach the Mother without taking the powerful hallucinogen. What if he could teach me to reach her in my dreams and have access to that fountain of knowledge whenever I wished? He said I would be able to ask her for guidance in all matters. He told me that he was in constant communion with entities that he relied on to guide him in his life. I had already made contact with her and he could teach me how to build a bridge in space-time and be able to go to her in my dreams. He told me that our whole life is but a dream. We have our sleeping dreams and our waking dreams. When we can master our sleeping dreams we can access knowledge that will help us in our waking dream. With that knowledge we can manipulate our waking dream into whatever we can envision.

I was hooked. I had suspected that there was much to be gained from using dreaming as a learning tool. Daniel said he would be hosting a small group of people at the Centre in November and he invited me to take part. I jumped at the chance to become the master of my dreams! The retreat was more than a month away, so Daniel gave me some rather vague directions to his compound and we agreed to meet there at the appointed time. I figured it was in the middle of the desert, how hard could it be to find. I think Daniel was of the opinion that if I found my way there, it was meant to be. If I could not find it, maybe that also was meant to be.

We parted ways with the agreement to meet in November in the high desert of San Luis Potosi. In the meantime, I would continue my exploration of the coast and its incredible beaches. I considered staying in San Pancho as I had come to love the quiet little beach town, but I felt a calling to see the places where I had spent time in my youth.

~•~

I continued my exploration of the Mexican Riviera, avoiding towns and camping in the deserted beaches when I could find them. I was working my way towards Manzanillo where I had spent an amazing year as a teen. This time spent exploring the coast was quite possibly the best time of my life! I lost all sense of time and just languished in the solitude of the impossibly beautiful playas, my only worries being my next meal.

One day as I was nearing my destination I passed a sign on the highway pointing to a place called Boca de Iguana. I vaguely remembered this place from all those many years ago and was not about to pass up another beach access. The short drive ended at the beach where there was a dilapidated trailer park, a deserted resort and a small store. Chapo and I got out to reconnoiter the beach and I was enamored with the remoteness of it. We were at one end of a small bay and I could see a small town at the other end, some five kilometers down the beach.

I decided to see if I could camp at the trailer park and was walking back to my truck when I passed an immaculate two-story house with a pool that I hadn't noticed. This was the only house at this end of the bay and, while walking by, I noticed a small sign saying "se rente." On a whim I decided to ask the pretty woman who was working in the yard if the place was for rent. It turned out that she was the owner and she said she usually rented it out by the week to people from Guadalajara and Mexico City. She was just cleaning up after some guests and I asked her if she would consider renting it for the month. She had no reservations lined up and said she would welcome a month-long renter as it would free her of her weekly job of cleaning for a while. She quoted me a price that I could not pass up, and just like that, I had my own personal beach with a small store for supplies right next door. I was in heaven! I could stay here until time to meet Daniel in the desert.

For the next couple of weeks I lived what I considered to be the idyllic life. I swam, fished and body surfed while Chapo frolicked in the waves and chased sea birds and crabs. Every other day or so we would walk the five kilometers along the beach to town for supplies that we couldn't get in the little store next door. Once, while walking past an open-air beachfront restaurant, we skirted close to a lagoon and we were astonished when the calm waters erupted.

A huge crocodile exploded from the water and narrowly missed having Chapo for breakfast! Luckily Chapo had super quick dog reflexes and he was just able to elude the monster's gaping jaws. We scrambled back to the beach, much to the amusement of the restaurants' patrons. I was not so amused and asked them why they hadn't warned us. These Mexicans had a rather cavalier attitude towards dogs and they informed me that this particular monster was somewhat of a pet and usually ate three or four stray dogs a year. I thanked them for the belated warning and walked back up the beach with a visibly shaken Chapo close on my heels. Chapo never really recovered from the scare and spent the remainder of our time there scrutinizing every patch of water for potential monstrous crocodiles.

About two weeks into our stay my health took a drastic turn south. I was stricken with a bad stomach ache that I initially passed off as a case of the dreaded Montezuma's Revenge. It wasn't long before I realized that this wasn't a case of severe diarrhea, it felt different. After several bad days I got a hold of my landlord who lived in Melaque some twenty kilometers south. She arranged for me to see her doctor who told me I had a stomach infection and prescribed a regimen of antibiotics. After another week of not being able to keep anything down I returned to the doctor and he gave me an IV and some different pills. The fluids helped, and I began to feel a bit better.

In another act of kindness, she let me stay in town at her bed and breakfast for free while I recovered. I regained some of my lost strength, but the discomfort in my stomach and lack of appetite remained. It was the middle of October and getting close to my rendezvous with Daniel when I took my leave and started heading into the mountains towards San Luis Potosi.

~•~

I allowed plenty of time to reach the retreat, which was a good thing, because I wasn't in the best of shape. My days were short and my diet not very good because I was leery of most roadside restaurants. I ate mostly fruit and yogurt, and soup when I could find it. I spent an especially bad night in a motel in Zacatecas the last night before reaching the Centre. In a feverish dream I could swear I heard my father, who had recently passed away, tell me everything was going to be alright.

The next morning, I felt worn-out and weak. When I had read about the retreat online it had mentioned that healers went to the Centre to refine their arts. I was hoping that Daniel or someone else there could be of more help than the doctors had been. When Chapo and I loaded up to go in search of Daniel's compound I was eager to get to a place where I could rest and recuperate.

We were in the high desert now. Daniel had told me that the Centre was located at the base of the Sierra de Catorce Mountains. It was mid-morning and starting to get hot when the mountain seemed to rise up out of the desert. When I first noticed her, she was still some 100 kilometers away. Even from a distance, there was something special about this mountain. She lorded over the sparse flat plains. I felt like my spirit was being drawn to her.

As we got closer, I had the vision of a crystal dance fleetingly thru my thoughts. As an avid believer in the power of crystals and a regular rock hound, I was forever on the lookout for them and this majestic mountain seemed to be offering the promise of one. Later, Daniel would tell us that the mountain is what had called us here. I had the feeling that she was alive, and if the Mother Ayahuasca had the ability to summon me, then maybe the mountain had done the same. Maybe, if I played my cards right, the mountain would offer me up one of her crystals. One can only hope.

Daniel's instructions were basically that you could see the distinctive igloos of the retreat from a place called Real Catorce, at the base of the mountain. The towns here were few and far between. I hoped it was that easy. I noticed a sign saying Real de Catorce pointing up a steep canyon and turned off the main road.

I headed up a fairly rough dirt road towards what looked like a huge canyon. As we climbed, it got cooler and greener. A good ways into the canyon I was surprised when I came around a bend and found an old mining village. This must be Real de Catorce! When I looked back down towards the desert I could not see any sign of the distinctive "igloos" of Daniel's compound. It was still early, and the town looked ancient and amazing, so I decided to explore a bit.

The old masonry buildings of the dying mining town clung to the mountainside. The people of the village seemed polite, but shy and reserved, when Chapo and I got out to admire the architecture. There was a familiar feeling like solo gringos were a bit of a curiosity here. We stretched and toured the narrow cobblestone streets. The mining town that was once a jewel seemed to be fading away now. The road continued up the mountain and I learned that there was a famous monastery somewhere at the top. The track was steep and narrow, but I thought it might be special and continued on past the village. As I climbed the road seemed to shrink and erode and I began to think that the monastery could wait for another time. The problem was there was no place to turn around! Twice we ran into jeeps full of pilgrims to the shrine which were barreling down the mountain at a ridiculous speed. By sheer luck, we barely avoided knocking each other off the cliff. Luckily, the jeep drivers didn't make me back down the mountain as my truck had a camper and that would not have been fun. They backed up far enough so that I could squeeze by them in a white knuckled sweat. The cliff wall was a shear drop by now.

The road turned washboard-like, and I noticed that I couldn't pry my fingers from the steering wheel. My death grip on the wheel relaxed slightly when I found a turnout to a goat farm that was perched precariously on the side of the cliff. By this time, Chapo and I needed a break and we got out of the truck to realize that the canyon was spectacular! I considered hiking the rest of the way up to the chapel, but had no idea how far it was. I could imagine the shrine hanging off the rocky cliffs of the summit. I was sure it must have been spectacular. Maybe it was a hike for another day. I certainly wouldn't be riding in one of the jeeps.

By now it was afternoon and I thought it was time to start looking for the retreat. Before I could very carefully turn my rig around to face downhill I was waved down by the resident shepherd. He asked me what a gringo was doing way out here. I told him I was looking for a retreat in the desert nearby. He told me that he was the guide to the peyote cactus in the area and that I didn't need a stupid retreat. He could take me to all the peyote I wanted. Judging by the glassiness of his gaze, his benefactor, the powerful peyote cactus had long ago gone from a medicine to the point where the plant was now his master. I knew that peyote was an integral part of the religion in this region of Mexico and I wondered about the spirit of this medicine. It seemed to me that these powerful medicines also had a very dark side to them. They were to be used only with respect or there could be consequences. These plants had spirits and disrespect could be perilous. I hadn't spoken with Daniel about whether or not he was going to hold a peyote ceremony. If I was going to be eating any of the powerful cactus medicine, it would be in a ceremony with someone who knew how to respect it. I declined the invitation for a peyote safari and asked if he knew where the retreat might be. He was disappointed with me and I got no help from him. It was time to go, so I gingerly road my brakes down the rugged dirt road towards the desert.

We made it back down to the paved road without further incidents, but I still had no clue where the retreat was. I continued in the direction that I had been going; looking for someone I could ask for directions. It wasn't long before I came on a cluster of buildings that wasn't big enough to be called a town, at least not on the map I had. As we got nearer, I saw a friendly looking guy wave at me, so I pulled over to ask him if he knew where the retreat was. He said his name was Juan and he knew exactly where it was. If I gave him some gas money he would lead me there. Juan seemed to be in an excellent mood. I just happened to have a gas can with me and as we filled his tank I found out why Juan was so happy. The door of his small adobe house opened and his wife and young son came out. She was carrying a couple of glasses and gave one to each of us saying we better drink it before the ride. Not recognizing the drink, I asked her what it was. She said it was special tea and beamed proudly at me. Not wanting to be rude, I took a drink. It was not like any tea I had ever tasted and they looked at me expectantly. I told her it was very good and she stood there waiting for me to finish it. As I drank it down, Juan explained to me that it was peyote tea and they drank it every day for strength. Oh great, I thought. I was going to show up at the retreat under the influence. I asked him if I was going to get high. He said not high just happy. I didn't really know what to say to all this. I just hoped he really could show me the way to Daniel's place. Luckily for me, the brew was not all that powerful, but I noticed I too was in a good mood the rest of the day.

Before long I was eating dust following Juan's truck down a very unused desert road that was right next to his house. It turned out that he could have just pointed out the road to me because it led straight to the retreat. It was only about a mile away. I guess Juan thought that a crazy gringo way out here could get lost out there in the desert. More likely, he had just needed some gas, but either way, he brought me straight to the Center of the Conscious Dream.

~•~

Daniel was in the middle of a game of cricket with some kids from the settlement back on the road. He paused the game to come over and thank Juan for his help. He pointed out where to park my truck and told me to make myself at home and pick out a hut to stay in. The compound consisted of a collection of huts arranged in a circle around a large open area with a fire-pit in the center. The huts were small, with room for one or two people, and built in the shape of igloos. One of the igloos was larger than the others and was used for ceremony. There were only five people staying here at the moment; Daniel and his son Venato, a couple from the nearby state of Guanajuato, and a young man from Daniel's home town of San Francisco. There were a couple of more conventional buildings used for common area and meetings, a kitchen and a couple of outhouses.

As I looked around I ran into the couple named Yei and Fanny. They were the kind of people that you instantly liked. I later found out that they were Temazcal leaders and Mexhica dancers. He was a desert plant expert and they ran a holistic healing center in Celaya, Guanajuato.

They spoke no English, and while I was once fluent in Spanish, that had been almost half a century ago, and in a previous lifetime. My Spanish was coming back but not as fast as I would have liked. Nevertheless, we got our points across. From what I understood, they were here in mourning because they had just lost a dog that was very special to them. In a rather bizarre coincidence, the t-shirt I was wearing had a drawing of a dog that looked exactly like the one he had just lost. This holy desert had a portal nearby that the Huichol Indians used to help their loved ones pass into the next life. It was also the destination of a yearly pilgrimage of some 300 miles made by the Huichols that started in Jalisco. The couple was here mourning their beloved dog passing and to help him find his way in the afterlife. I have lost dogs before and know how devastating it is.

As soon as I picked out my hut and got my stuff settled I changed my shirt and went to find them. When I offered the dog shirt to him, he looked astonished, and we became friends. They were only here for a week but, in that time, they would teach me many things and help me with my stomach ailments. They were intelligent, vibrant and spiritual. They had the glow that only people who are truly content can have. They were powerful and in the prime of their lives and beautiful to behold. They had such reverence for the desert and seemed in tune with their surroundings in a way I had never really experienced. With very few words they showed me what it looked like to live a life that was in harmony with the world. They seem to have made a huge impression on me because I think of them often and I hope that someday I can achieve the bond that they had with the Earth.

I sat and watched Daniel play ball with the kids with the Mountain looming nearby. The Mountain seemed to have a presence. This whole place had the same feel that I had in the Sacred Valley. There was a holy and slightly surreal feeling that made you want to whisper. The Mountain was the source of the energy. She had created one of those vortexes of power that drew people in, like Sedona, Chaco Canyon or Machu Picchu. The Mountain lay to the east of the retreat and she shaded the camp in the early morning from first rays of the rising sun. We were blessed with cool, misty and even sleepy mornings. A very pleasant way to greet what would invariably be a blistering day. In the evenings she was an ebony castle lit up with little diamonds of light from the mining camps that littered her slopes. For the next three weeks the Mountain would provide a magical place to learn some of the mysteries I sought and she would prove to be an incredible teacher. I had that special feeling you get when you know that you had made the right decision and you are exactly where you are supposed to be, doing exactly what you were intended to be doing.

~•~

Daniel ran a very informal and relaxed retreat. The kitchen was simple with a stove, a pantry and a table. We were responsible for our own breakfast which we made with food from the pantry. Our bathing would be done from a bucket. We would be living at a basic level and there were few distractions.

Daniel had contracted with a local family to provide the evenings meals for us and they also stocked the pantry with food for our breakfast and mid-day meals.

The evening meals were an array of local cuisine made up mostly of soups and vegetables with occasional different meat entrees. Reasonable requests were honored, but we eagerly looked forward to each of the evening meals. This was the exact type of food my body needed at that time. During my stay at the retreat my strength gradually returned.

There was no real time-table of activities so, after everyone had risen and eaten, we cleaned up after ourselves and began to gather under a large Palo Verde tree which was our morning meeting place. Daniel was invariably the last to get up and the four of us were quietly getting to know each other when he joined us under the tree.

We were all here for different reasons and I was the only one that spoke English so my first week in camp was pretty much a crash course in conversational Spanish. I followed as best I could but was often left behind. Daniel spoke English to me.

It was under the tree where Daniel would tell us what we needed to know about the daily retreat routines, take food requests, and run messages if needed. There were no cell phones here. Daniel discouraged any alcohol or substance abuse. He would also listen to our dreams. There was something about this camp under the gaze of the powerful Mountain that seemed to facilitate vivid dreams. I was of the hope that Daniel could teach me to master mine.

After hearing our progress, he would set a task for each of us. Since we were all here for different reasons, our tasks were also different. One of the tasks Daniel set for the others was to go for days at a time without speaking. This also put a thorn in our conversations. I came to realize that Daniel preferred we not spend a lot of time talking. We could do that anywhere. We were here to work. Talking about trivial things and current events not having to do with the retreat was discouraged. He was trying to get us to leave those things behind and to live in the moment. It was a good lesson to learn and live by. As a result, most of our conversations were about our spiritual journeys and the progress of our tasks. It seemed to intensify the air of spirituality and magic of this spot and served to focus our intent. This was no casual joke of a retreat. We were here to learn and if we did not take it seriously, Daniel would ask us to leave. He demanded that we respect him and our surroundings. I was impressed and excited.

I was still weak and having trouble eating so Daniel was going to speak with the women who prepared the meals about having lots of soup and steamed vegetables for me. There was also lots of fruit around. Just what I needed.

Since I was having trouble with food, Daniel told me that there are many ways to get sustenance. He talked to me about energy. All things whether alive or innate, contain energy. All matter is made of atoms and atoms are in perpetual motion. Even rocks are in motion and vibrate at a certain frequency. I flashed back to Machu Picchu and first feeling the vibration of the earth and the walls of the fortress.

Daniel told me he would take care of my food needs, but my task for the day was to go into the desert and try to take in sustenance from nature. The sun, the trees and all things living emit energy in one form or the other. It was possible to draw in the energy that surrounds us. As was Daniel's nature, he did not provide a lot of information about how to accomplish this. He would let me make an attempt and listen to my report on my return. If he wasn't satisfied with my effort he might offer suggestions, but he would tell me to do it again until he was.

I loaded up with enough water for Chapo and myself, grabbed some apples and oranges and we set off into the desert. I have always been a creature of the sun. I crave sunlight and am not happy when deprived of it. From sunlight I know how to draw energy, but I was not so sure about drawing it from nature.

This desert was very similar to the one I was accustomed to, but when I looked deeper there were many differences. First, I noticed that the Palo Verde trees had slightly different leaves. The cacti were slightly different cousins. The birds and insects were similar but different. What first appeared to be a familiar desert was actually very different.

Daniel had said to try and draw energy from the flowers. At first glance there were no flowers in sight. As I slowed down and became more immersed in my surroundings, I started noticing the tiny flowers that these desert plants hid very well. I surmised that they must camouflage their flowers as they would be a delicacy to most desert wildlife.

I still had no idea how to draw energy from such a fragile source.

I ended up finding fourteen different types of blooms, most of which I would never have noticed without searching. As I studied the blooms and noticed their differences, I became aware of their distinct smells. Not only did they have unique aromas, each blossom and each plant had its own kind of personality. Some thriving on the strong desert sun and others, hiding in the deepest shadows. As I became aware of their personalities I also sensed that each one evoked a different emotion within me. Each one had a distinct vibration. Each was vibrating at its own special frequency. I wasn't quite sure, but it seemed to me that it was by means of these frequencies that the flowers released their energy. They also were the source of nectar and it was incredible to watch how they contributed to the survival of all the other creatures of this magical desert.

By the time it took me to figure all this out it was already late in the day. As I was returning to the Centre I came across a shepherd on a horse with his flock. He rode up to me and asked if I had anything to eat. I gave him an apple and he asked what I was doing out here. I told him I was trying to get to know the desert. He thought that was about the funniest thing he had ever heard. He almost fell off his horse in a fit of laughter. Finally, he said, "Well, good luck with that, my friend!" and rode off chuckling about loco gringos.

Dinner was a delicious soup that I managed to keep down. Daniel seemed pleased with my day's efforts. Although he always seemed to be appraising me, often with an amused glint in his eye, he didn't have a lot to say. I surmised that if he didn't make me redo my task, then he was probably satisfied with my progress.

And so it went, there was no schedule and the time was only told by the rising and setting of the sun. Each morning Daniel would set me on a task that I very rarely understood until way later. With the excellent food and the suggestions other healers presented I started to regain my strength.

The others were here to let things go. They were tasked to not speak for days at a time and I would see them going off into the desert with shovels or musical instruments or whatnot. One evening, towards the end of their stay, Daniel said they were going to have a fire ceremony to help let souls and attachments pass onto where they were intended to go. He invited me to attend.

Fire ceremonies are very powerful tools for a shaman. In this ceremony Daniel would invoke the spirits of the earth, wind, fire, water, sun, moon, and the powerful mountain. He would then open a portal for the souls to pass. This desert was a vortex that attracted lost souls and he considered it his work to help them pass. Preparations for a fire ceremony can take all day; my task was to find some wood in the sparse desert.

My companions were healers and very spiritual people who were experienced in ceremony. Daniel is an amazing musician with a powerful voice. When he performs it has much the same effect as the magical Icaros sung by the shamans in Peru. This was my first fire ceremony and I was amazed and unprepared for the power and energy that Daniel and the other healers were able to harness. The ceremony took on the surreal quality that I had experienced in the Maloca in Peru although there were no healing plants involved in this ceremony. At one point, the others seemed to take on a glow as if they had somehow become angelic. Daniel's music wove a spell and we would drum or rattle along with him. Daniel told us each to take a turn and sing to show our sincerity and intent. The others were strong spiritual leaders in their own right and I was but a novice at this. I was not sure I even belonged here with these beings of light who were weaving a powerful spell and was terrified to sing for them. When it came my turn, I had no idea what or how to contribute and was astounded when something like a song or chant seemed to well up from within me. I felt as if something had taken control of me and I had no idea where the words had come from or in what language I had sung. I was astonished by what had happened, but the others continued as if nothing was out of sort. The ceremony went on, but I remember little of it, and what I did remember was dream-like. In the morning I told the young couple that they had become beings of light and that their songs and the ceremony had been beautiful. I hoped that I hadn't ruined anything by my ignorance and awkwardness. They laughed and told me that we had all been shining and yes it had been a beautiful and powerful ceremony. The power and presence of the Mountain made ceremonies here especially potent.

The next day the couple and their young friend departed and a new group arrived. There were also three in this group; a pretty young woman from Colorado named

Angelina, an ageless woman from Scotland named Tess and a quiet man from England named Marco. Again, I was moved by these peoples' courage to come so far to an unknown land in search of knowledge. Now we would begin our lessons in conscious dreaming.

The daily routine was similar to the previous week. In the mornings we would gather under the tree and review our dreams and the previous day's experiences. Daniel was an easy-going mentor with a great sense of humor. He would listen to our stories with great interest, often making funny comments or suggestions. There was no stress here, the only anxiety being whether we were up to the tasks that Daniel set for us. These tasks were designed to help us expand our consciousness in our waking dream.

In the evenings Daniel would instruct us in the art of conscious dreaming. He would do this with meditation exercises, informal lectures and musically. Listening to Daniel play his music was intoxicating. His music was a catalyst that could transport. When he played and sang my soul would take to flight! If you could surrender to its magic, it could take you places. Daniel's hypnotic music and voice worked with the power of the Mountain and combined to have a similar effect as that of Ayahuasca. While Mother Ayahuasca would show you things whether you were willing or not, Daniel's spell was more of an invitation. You had to let go and follow where it would lead. It reminded me of following the Shaman Angela's Icaros and how she would lead me with her song.

~•~

One of the first tasks that Daniel set for me was to go into the desert and make a personal medicine wheel. His medicine wheel philosophy was based on Mayan beliefs. This involved walking until I found a spot that resonated with me. Using that spot as the center of my wheel, I would walk North until I found a stone that moved me in some way. If it felt right when I held it to my heart, I would return to my wheel and place it to the North. North is the direction of the element Air and is associated with thought processes. Next, I would walk East until I found an appropriate stone. East is the element of Fire and is related to one's spirit and passion. Then I would go South, the element of Earth, which has to do with the physical body. West is to Water, it is the element of emotion. Believe it or not, this was not an easy task. There were not many stones in this part of the desert, let alone ones that moved me. Once I had trouble finding my way back to my wheel. The sun was high and hot, and I was tired and thirsty by the time I had my stones placed.

The trick was to open to the elements contained in the stones. I chose to sit quietly, clear my thoughts and open to the vibration of the Earth, much as I had in Machu Picchu. Once I felt calm and at one with the desert, I asked myself how I related to the elements of Air, Fire, Earth and Water. Which element had the strongest pull on me? My medicine wheel was completely out of balance and I almost toppled to the South, the element of the Earth. My physical being was in crisis! I tried to connect with that element to see if I could find what the cause of my physical distress was. The overwhelming answer to my question was Nutrition! My body was crying out for sustenance. Fortunately, I was being taken care of in that regard. I vowed that I was going to start eating even if it wasn't easy. There is one thing in life that is so basic that it is easy to take for granted, and that is hunger. Some see it as a cause for alarm, but I see it as a sign of life. If you do not have it in your life it is easy to forget just what a huge motivation it is. It is the driving force in life - our primal urge. Throughout the years of my illness it has been something that I had been often without. Lack of hunger will eventually wear you down. It is just hard to keep up your energy, your goals and your outlook on life. My hunger was a big part of who I was and I knew that I needed it to thrive. If I learned nothing else that day, it was that I needed to find my hunger! They may seem to be strange bedfellows, but believe you me; it is hard to be happy when you are not hungry.

Daniel showed me that sunrise and sunset are the times to pay homage and take nourishment from the sun. It is the only time we can lay eyes on him without harm. He taught me to stand quietly with my palms out and to take in his strength. You can also close your eyes and see a different version of the sunset, shifting your reality. This is the time to feel the breeze and hear the songs of the birds. With practice, you can let the sun's rays cleanse you of those things that are clinging to you. Once you have let go mentally, you can begin to let go of the physical aches and pains that have built up. Daniel had his own version of yoga, and once he shared it with me, I was hooked. It was simply to start to move gently and to just listen to your body. Your body knows what it needs and it will guide you. The key is to keep a slow steady pace and to keep a free flow of non-stop movement. If you just listen to your body, you will be surprised at the contortions it will talk you into.

~•~

One morning while meeting under the tree, I found out why I had seen the others walking into the desert with shovels. Daniel wanted us to pair up, go into the desert and dig a grave. Then one of us was to get naked and lie in the grave while the other buried them up to the neck. While buried, we were to tell the other person the story of our lives. I thought, wow, ok. Since we had all just met it seemed prudent that we paired off with someone of the same sex. Daniel had other thoughts and he instructed me to go with Angelina and Tess to go with Marco. I could sense right away that Angelina was not comfortable with this, but being the brave and adventurous spirit that she was, she agreed. I tried to reassure her that we would work it out. We gathered what we would need and went into the desert feeling a bit uneasy about the whole thing.

We walked until Angelina found the spot where she wanted to be buried. I dug the shallow grave and left her so that that could have some privacy. She lay down and did her best to cover herself in the soil. When she called I came back and finished the job, burying her so that just her head was exposed. She had a moment of panic when I got to her neck and I tried to calm her as best I could. She then told me the story of her life. Afterwards, I again gave her some privacy while she rose from her grave. The next day it was her turn to bury me.

This may sound bizarre and, at the time, we were also confused as to the purpose of this exercise. All I can tell you is that it is very similar to being reborn. When Angelina arose from her grave she looked like a new person. She wandered off into the desert like she had never seen one before. She told me she felt like a snake that had shed her skin.

I found the experience to be very similar to Peru when the Mother Ayahuasca had cleansed me with her dance. It was very liberating, and I too, felt like I had left unwanted thoughts and feelings behind me in the grave. It was a very special way to really get to know Angelina and we are fast friends to this day. That day in the desert I was given a new sister and we have a bond that goes beyond years and will undoubtedly last a lifetime. I will always have a special place in my heart for Angelina.

~•~

The tasks that Daniel set were beyond my understanding, so I was not surprised to hear him say that he wanted me to search out a tree that called to me and try to meditate with her. He said that trees are powerful teachers and have unique wisdom. I was a little intimidated by his request because I had never tried to commune with a tree before. By this time, the desert and the Mountain had me in their spell, and I set out with the thought that anything was possible and, maybe, this would be my time.

I grabbed a couple of apples and a drum and called my faithful friend Chapo. Daniel had told me to bring my smudge stick and make an offering to the tree. I took a gallon of water thinking; what tree doesn't like water?

Chapo and I set off on another adventure that was beyond our understanding, eager to see what magic this day would bring.

We started walking in an indiscriminate direction, wandering out into the vast desert looking for a friendly tree. The desert was serene and surreal in its magic and, by this time, I felt close to its creatures. I let Chapo be my guide; this was a job that he relished.

I saw my tree from a distance and knew instinctively that she was right for me. She swayed majestically in the breeze above her sisters and their daughters. She towered over her siblings and children and their children! I had found the mother tree of this part of the desert.

From my pack I removed my smudge stick and circled her with it. I spoke to her of my desire to learn the mysteries of the desert. I implored her to speak with me. I told her that I was but an ignorant human with no knowledge of her universe. I humbly asked her to take pity on my ignorance and bless me with her experience.

I then sprinkled water around her perimeter saying that I realized that it was but a token, but that I hoped it pleased her. I introduced myself and tried to get to know her. I cleaned the deadfall from her base and began climbing her branches and picking off some parasitic growths that seemed to me to be bothering her. In my explorations, I found a comfortable crook in the arms of her branches and made myself at ease. Chapo, not once doubting his friend's intentions, lay down at her base and patiently settled in to wait.

I started with my breathing. For me, everything starts with the miracle of the life-giving breath. I closed my eyes and started drumming in rhythm with my breath and my beating heart. I was aware of my contact with the tree and I felt every groove of her bark where my body touched hers. Slowly, I began to feel a vibration coming from the tree. The rhythm of my breath and drum altered to come in sync with her vibrations. My skin began to harden like bark and I imagined that I was becoming one with her. I lost all sense of time and ego and, at some point, she accepted me, and I fell back into her and was absorbed into her world.

An immense sense of strength and maturity and boundless love washed over me and I thought I could intuit meaning in her vibrations. With astonishment, I realized that she was singing to me! It was a song of the ages! It was her song and she was singing me a lullaby which told her tale. She was old. As old as can be remembered. And she was the Mother tree. She was the first and the strongest of her tribe and she took me on a tour of her world. She showed me how she was the creator and center of her own cosmos!

She let me see a portion of her universe. It started in the depths of the earth. Her taproot cleaved past the hard soil, caliche and packed stones to where the desert's blood ran. There was a river far below us and she drew nectar from the depths and raised it to the sun to magically transform it into energy and air!

She sang to me of the ecosystem that she had created and the diversity of life she supported. She was the source of life for the crawling creatures such as ants, beetles and spiders that used her for sustenance and shelter to their winged cousins - the bees and butterflies. The birds came to feed on the insects and to spread her seeds. She was their ward, and without her, there could be no existence.

I realized that she was indeed the Mother! This matriarch had created and nurtured an incredible, living, and evolving ecosystem. She drew water and nutrients from the depths and transformed them into a whole world of diversity and wonders! With her magic, she created the air that sustains all her children. In the evenings she sang to the stars! Without her, the desert would be devoid of life. I came to the realization that I too was her child as she gently returned me to what I call my reality. I began to see that she was trying to teach me something basic about how life worked. There was something that she sensed was out of kilter with my body and she was trying to make me aware of it. With a feeling of love, she sent me on my way with one last admonishment. GO EAT SOMETHING!

I made my way back to camp secure in the knowledge that I had another mother; not one, but many! There is a bond between ourselves and nature that we can ignore, but not break! If we break this bond, we destroy ourselves!

My new-found Mother would be there for me in my time in the desert. She was wise beyond knowing and ruled by love! She would help me to understand myself, some of the mysteries of the desert and Daniel's teachings. Her knowledge and capacity for love and the fact that she had adopted this ignorant human into her fold gave me hope and a fierce desire to protect and appreciate her and the world she had created! I have never been able to make contact with another tree as I did with her. Perhaps she was a magical tree in an enchanting place. I am now often drawn to trees. I crave their touch and their gentle and peaceful nature. It is always a pleasure to be able to sit quietly and appreciate what they have to offer. Without the trees we would not have our life-giving breath because there would be no air to breathe!

~•~

While we were lounging under the meeting tree one afternoon I asked Daniel about something that had been bothering me for a while. I told him about a hike Chapo and I had taken once while visiting my sister in San Carlos. It was the hot season in San Carlos and we had started early to avoid the nearly dangerous afternoon sun. The air was hot and humid and plant life this time of year was thick and obscuring the path. Several times I had to backtrack when I hit obstacles that threatened to end my hike before I was ready. If I didn't find a way through soon I would have to turn back. Even if I was lucky enough to get through, I was beginning to worry about how much water was left in my bottle.

For some strange reason, I felt drawn to whatever lay beyond the dense vegetation and narrowing canyon. At one point, I was stopped by a thick wall of cactus mixed with all manner of other vicious looking plants. I was stymied and discouraged and sat down to cool off in the shade of the canyon wall. As I cooled I scanned the walls of the canyon. I thought I saw the faintest of ledges that ran along the wall above the tops of the deadly looking foliage. It was just barely noticeable and looked hard to get to, but I was reluctant to turn back, because I had a strange feeling that there was something special up there if I could just get through.

I boosted Chapo up to the ledge and he scrambled along and then seemed to vanish around a bend. I followed as best I could with my back against the steep canyon wall. As I made my way cautiously along the narrow shelf I could hear Chapo enthusiastically urging me to hurry. The ledge narrowed even more and I was just about to give up when I was bailed out by some hidden handholds carved into the cliff face. I edged around a corner and was surprised to see an amazing hidden valley surrounded by hillsides.

The hair on the back of my neck began to tingle and I felt a familiar feeling of an ancient presence in the air. My instincts were quickly confirmed as I found bits of worked stone and shards of pottery lying about. It wasn't long before I noticed a pile of oyster and conch shells. This was a confirmation that people had once come to this hidden sanctuary bringing seafood harvested from the coast a few miles to the west.

Sifting through the shells, I noticed a few obsidian flakes and my heart quickened. Within minutes, I found among the many shells, five of the most impeccably crafted obsidian arrowheads that I had ever seen! I was astonished and deeply humbled. I sat stunned considering my blessings! These were exquisite pieces and I had found five of them in one spot!

Because of the remoteness of this place and how difficult it was to access, I had a feeling no one had been here for many years. Sitting there, examining these incredible relics, I considered the implications of my findings. It was obvious that this place had not been visited by people since being abandoned by its original inhabitants. I tried to fathom why anyone would discard these perfect works of art. As I continued my explorations, I could not shake the feeling of being watched. I was used to being among the ancient spirits and they usually went about their business without acknowledging me. This seemingly peaceful hidden enclave was beginning to make me uneasy. There was a malevolent presence in the air and I had a distinct feeling that I was not wanted here.

Although I was beginning to feel intimidated, I was also buoyed by my recent finds and eager to see what other mysteries were hidden here. I cautiously continued to explore. The valley was ringed by hills and effectively hidden from view. From the surrounding desert it was completely undetectable.

The far end of the valley terminated abruptly at a gorge. I followed the gorge uphill to its source and came to a small waterfall. There was a small stream issuing from a spring higher up on the slope of the cliff. As the stream trickled down the slope it dropped into a series of amazing jacuzzi-like pools before reaching the waterfall and falling into the gorge below. This hidden valley was incredible, and I could see why the Indians would have been attracted to this place. It had a rare source of water in this arid landscape. Being parched from the hike, I immediately stripped and followed Chapo into one of the pools. The water was cool and refreshing and I couldn't help but notice the stark beauty of this place and the strong vibrations that seemed to be trapped here. I wondered about the people who had lived here and why they had chosen to move on from this enchanting hideaway.

Being refreshed and exhilarated, I felt ready to go back and show my friends my amazing finds! As I worked my way back to the hidden valley, I heard a raucous commotion on the cliff opposite the gorge. To my astonishment, there was a huge hawk harrowing a mountain lion that was descending towards me across the gorge. I stood silently as they made their way down the cliff. The hawk was rowdily harassing the big cat and was being rudely ignored.

I was mesmerized and paralyzed in place as they came to a stop directly across the gorge from me. I wasn't afraid and did not feel particularly threatened, as the gorge was easily fifty feet deep and had sheer sides. The majestic cat crouched down and stared at me across the void while his noisy friend perched in a saguaro above his head.

I was hypnotized by this spectacle and have no idea how long we sat there contemplating each other. Finally, the huge feline got up and stretched luxuriously. She seemed to be looking for a way to come across the gorge! Oh shit! I was sure she realized that she could cross above the waterfall. I felt an urgent need to be elsewhere when she got to this side. It was time for me to beat a hasty retreat! Chapo and I eased back into the remarkable little valley until we were out of her sight before turning and I raced Chapo out of the canyon. I had a suspicion that the cat was way faster than we were and I had no intention of being the first to be caught. The mountain lion had either not been hungry or had just wanted to scare us out of her territory and we emerged from the canyon unscathed.

After relating my story to Daniel I explained to him that ever since I was a youngster I have had the innate ability to find ancient Indian sites. If I was fortunate enough to find a relic or something that they may have left behind, I would treasure it and display it so that someone else might appreciate it. I do not do this lightly. I have never dug or disrespected a site. If I have the good fortune to find something on the surface I consider it a great blessing, and always thought it better to save them than leave them to be forgotten.

Many months had now passed and, while I still felt blessed by my experience, I was a bit unsettled about it. I felt as if I had missed something. I could still feel the big cat's cold gaze and hear the hawk's admonishments. I told Daniel that I had never been uneasy about removing artifacts from a site before and that I still felt a sense that I had done something wrong and that the cougar and the raptor had been trying to tell me something.

Daniel suggested that this might be a good exercise in dreaming with intent. He suggested that I go back in my dreams and try to connect and figure out what I had missed. When I asked him just how I was supposed to accomplish going back there in a dream, he told me that I had made an important connection with a very wise sorceress and that maybe she could help me. He was referring to the Mother tree that had seemed to adopt me.

So, before bedtime, in the twilight of a near full moon, I gathered Chapo and my essentials and made my way to her to seek her guidance. The desert was cool and quiet, and she loomed tall in the half light. I greeted her in my usual way with smudging and an offering of water and settled at her trunk and began to drum. My connection with her was strong and before long she accepted me, and I again entered her world. My senses were flooded with an unconditional love and, in that moment, I was able to ask her for her guidance in my attempt at dreaming with the intent of going back to the magical hidden valley in San Carlos. While she gave me no sign or instruction, I felt an onset of confidence in my abilities and a sudden weariness. She was urging me to go do my dreaming. She had work to do. This night she would be singing to the stars! When I left her, I felt calm and undaunted by my task. We made our way back to camp and I lay down on my mat and was instantly asleep.

I was aware of crawling into my hut in one instance and staring across the gorge into the ferocious eyes of the mountain lion the next. I was there! I was back in the hidden valley with the cougar and her hawk friend eagerly stating her opinion. I could feel the great cat's animosity towards me. She was not pleased that I was again trespassing in her domain! She rose out of her crouch and slashed at me with her enormous paw.

Suddenly, she was gone, and I felt a menacing presence behind me. I turned around and was looking into the eyes of one of the most terrifying individuals I have ever seen!

Before me stood a beautiful, terrible and frightening apparition! He was majestic in his terribleness! His fierce eyes bored into me and I had a gut feeling of total inadequacy. He was shorter than me but towered over me in his power. I became aware that his beauty was marred with dirt and nasty mortal looking wounds.

As I stood trembling before him, he addressed me with disdain and, to my astonishment, I learned I could understand him. He asked me why I had returned to this sacred place.

I told him that I had not been aware that this place was sacred to his people when I removed the arrowheads and that I was here to attempt to make amends. For what seemed an eternity he regarded me solemnly and I could feel him peeling away the layers of my soul seeking the truth in my words. I nervously awaited his judgment. Finally, he nodded his head and told me that he did not have a problem with me admiring their mastery of flint work and wanting to possess something from a culture that I revered. What he did have a problem with was that I had intruded not once, but twice into the most holy of places for his people. It was not alright that I had found this hidden valley and it was not okay that I had returned. He went on to show me why. In a vision, with awful clarity, he showed me why this was a sacred place to his people. It left me reeling and sick to the depths of my soul.

His was a band of two hundred mighty warriors and their families. These fiercely proud people had kept the Spanish invasion of their world at bay for fifty years. They had sacked and burned the first two missions sent to enslave them. The once numerous tribe had been whittled down by war and accompanying hardships that went with battling a relentlessly greedy adversary.

He went on to show how one day his once mighty tribe was dismayed to see a great fleet of winged sea serpents bearing an evil army of soldiers sailing into their harbor. As the awful plague disembarked by the hundreds on their once pristine shores, the holy men of the tribe realized that they were looking at their tribe's demise. They retreated to this, their most sacred place to await the onslaught of evil that was descending upon them.

He gave me a vision of his sleeping village that had been surrounded in the night by the emissaries of the devil bearing Christian crosses. The scene played out and I watched horrified as these creatures of darkness and cowardice descended on his sleeping tribe. I was in the middle of a terrible battle where every last man, woman and child was slaughtered in their sleep or died trying to defend their loved ones.

The vile soldiers left the hidden valley full of the bloody corpses of a once proud people. I was appalled and sickened by the vision. I now understood his animosity and wondered that he didn't just kill me out of spite. In the centuries since the massacre, Mother Earth had reverently buried their people with sand blown in from the desert. I, on the other hand, had unknowingly trampled their graves.

I bowed my head to my beautiful apparition and conveyed the sorrow I felt for his tribe and my clumsiness. I told him I was being tortured for what I had done. I expressed that I held his people in the highest esteem and that I regretted not being born to his tribe and not having died alongside these ancestors that I held above all others. I told him that he had fought courageously and that I envied his honorable death.

His fierce eyes melted into sorrow as he regarded me silently. Then he put his fist to his heart and said he wished I had been there also. He said that before I could be forgiven for my trespasses he had a task for me. He wanted me to sanctify this holy ground as there had been no one left to do it for them. I told him it would be one of the most meaningful things I could do in my pitiful life. I would be honored!

He told me to gather firewood and pile it in huge mounds at the four cardinal corners. He then showed me specific plants to gather and sprinkle around the perimeter of the village. I toiled endlessly in this sorrowful dreamscape. In the end I was as dirty and bloody as my proud apparition.

I was instructed to light the fires, and in their light, I noticed that we weren't alone. The rest of his tribe began appearing and making their way to a place I had cleared in the center of the village. They were splendid in their costume dress and thankfully showed no signs of their wounds. As they gathered in the clearing I began to hear the beat of drums and at once the whole tribe burst into motion in an intoxicating dance. I watched as these handsome people celebrated their lives and deaths. The colors of their costumes and the intricate movements of their dance bear no description.

I stood with tears flowing down my face as one by one the members of this once powerful people passed by me and seemed to vanish into the night. Soon I was alone with my benefactor. He stood erect and he was impressive now that his wounds were gone, and he was in his ceremonial garb. After a time, he reached out and clasped my hand and pulled me to his chest. Without another word he nodded and faded away.

When I awoke the next day I lay in my hut and pondered my amazing dream. I examined myself for cuts and bruises. So real was the dream that I remembered every part of it. Slowly, I realized that I had done it! I had somehow been able to travel to that distant place and be an active participant in the dream. At the time, I was unaware that this would turn out to be the single, most important night of my life. It would forever change the way I looked at and approached my life. A paradigm had shifted in my reality! The line between my dreams and my waking world was getting blurry.

It was while lying in my little hut on a cold and misty morning that I first realized that my whole life was a dream. And the scary part was, I didn't even know if it was MY dream! What if I was just a part of someone else's dream? It was then that I began to realize that, if I could control my sleeping dreams, then surely, I could control my waking dreams as well. At the time, I had no idea how this realization would change my life. Suffice it to say that it was Daniel's greatest gift to me and for that I owe him a debt I fear that I can never repay.

I found that the big cat no longer prowled my conscience. I was no longer troubled by the thought of collecting an artifact from the ancestors that I held in reverence. I hoped I had brought peace to those tortured souls and that they could now sleep in peace. I also hope that no one else ever has cause to find that hidden valley and disturb their rightful slumbers. I made a vow to myself that if I ever returned to San Carlos, I would return to the hidden valley and repeat the ceremony in the flesh.

~•~

Chapo let me know that it was time to go out and greet the morning. I wondered if the others would recognize me this morning. I certainly felt changed and I would not have doubted if I looked differently also.

My companions were waiting for me under the meeting tree that morning as I was late. To my relief, no one laughed, winced or made the sign of the cross when I approached. Apparently, I did not look any different. Daniel was appraising me with a bemused look, but that was nothing new to me. I tried to explain the miracle of what I had experienced and failed miserably. I gave up when I realized that I didn't have the words. It was impossible for me to explain when I didn't fully understand what had transpired myself.

Daniel announced that it was time that we tried to meet our animal spirit guides. He explained that animal guides can help us navigate our daily lives. An animal has no doubt as to its place in the world, whereas people on the other hand are riddled with ambiguity and indecisiveness and often lose their way. A person can have more than one animal guide and can have many in their lifetime. Daniel explained how to open ourselves to the spirit world and ask our guides to reveal themselves to us.

I was elated! I had always wondered about and wanted to meet my spirit guide! From my previous experiences in this surreal desert, I knew exactly where to go. If anyone could help me find my animal guide it would be the Mother tree of the desert! I grabbed my pack, some fruit, water, drum and my smudge stick and set off in search of knowledge. Chapo led the way to my tree Mother; he also knew where to go.

I greeted her with prayer. I smudged her perimeter asking for her blessings. As I sprinkled my offering of water to her I asked that she guide me in my quest to find the animal spirit who guides me. I did some general maintenance around her and then settled at her trunk. Chapo, who usually had business of his own, settled down right next to me. I found this kind of odd, but figured that maybe he wanted a say in who my animal guide was, him being my best friend and all.

I cleared my mind and started drumming. With my breathing, I tried to match the vibrations being emitted from the tree. Once I felt that we were in rhythm, I asked again that she help me find my guide. I cast out invitations to the universe. I tried to see the world through my third eye and I opened my mind and put forth a summons. I pleaded with the animal spirits to introduce themselves to me.

Soon fleeting images of different animals began to flitter through my mind's eye. I had brief visions of hawks, then badgers and wolves, but they moved on. My attention waned. I surfaced and noticed that Chapo was still right by my side and was giving me an oddly intense look.

After a respite I tried again. Drumming. Breathing. Becoming one with the vibrations of my Mother and the

Earth. This time as I sent out my intentions I was repeatedly distracted. First, my concentration was shattered by the snap of a breaking branch. As I tried again, I was startled by the sound of a rock landing next to me.

That was enough. Someone or something was surely messing with me. I got up and walked around looking for the culprit. Chapo was glued to my side and looking around nervously. That was unusual for my free-spirited friend. My search was in vein and I returned to the tree and sat down. It was hot and I was discouraged and I may have dozed off in the heat. My reverie was broken by something that sounded like a "yip." When I opened my eyes, the desert seemed to have a surreal quality to it. I was confused and not sure I was fully awake. This was another example of how the lines between my dreams and my waking world were becoming blurred. I was starting to question my sanity. I realized that each of us has their own reality and that mine might never again fit into the box that most people considered normal. Surprisingly, this thought caused me no alarm and I was even relieved that I had finally escaped from the clutches of conventional thinking.

I was in the same desert. I was still sitting under my Mother tree with Chapo, although he was again giving me a rather intense doggy stare. Everything was the same but different. It was as if I had entered a parallel dimension.

Chapo and I got up and started to look around. We walked into the desert and I heard Chapo issue a challenge. When I looked down I noticed that his hackles were raised. This was unusual for my easygoing dog. When I looked up again I saw the reason for his alarm.

We were half surrounded by a pack of coyotes who were issuing a challenge of their own! We all stood transfixed, staring at each other. Chapo was still growling and the coyotes looked hungry, mean, amused and seemed ready to fight or play.

After an eternal moment, the biggest beast stepped forward and words seemed to blossom in my head.

"Well, well. The hard-headed one has woken up. We have been trying to get your attention for a while. First you plead for help and then, when we come, you are too blind to see us. There you are sleeping under the Mother and guarded by your Protector, we were about to leave you to your slumbers."

"I can show you some things if you aren't too blind and lazy to keep up. I don't know about him," he glared at Chapo.

Chapo is not a big dog, but he has a HUGE heart and has no idea how to be afraid. Chapo and I have no problems understanding each other, so when I asked him if he could keep up with his distant cousins, his grin was all I needed to know.

I told the Alfa that we would do our best, and just like that, we were part of the pack. They descended on us and there was much sniffing and licking and wagging of tails. Abruptly, with a signal from the boss the pack moved off into the desert with Chapo and me following as best we could.

The coyotes went about their business of hunting, cavorting and basically looking for any kind of mischief they could find. They kept a brisk pace and, when I began to tire, the Alfa came back to me shaking his head. Again, his thoughts were clear to me. They said that I was weak and he feared I had forgotten how to have fun. By now the sun was at its peak and the pack were at their dens where they would rest during the worst of the heat.

The leader intuited that it was time to get out of the sun and that I now knew where to find him if I ever wanted to play. He disappeared into his den and Chapo and I were left standing alone in the desert.

It had been a fascinating glimpse into the lives of these wily desert dwellers. They were fierce hunters. They were intelligent and inquisitive and, yes, they knew how to have a good time. I had learned much about this place by watching their antics.

When I looked around, I realized that I was lost. Fortunately for me, I had a dog with me that rarely lost his way and the great mountain was an unmistakable landmark. We walked in the direction of the mountain and after a couple of miles I saw the familiar outline of the Mother tree in the distance.

I was stopped dead in my tracks by the thought that Chapo and I had traveled miles in my dream, or vision, or whatever that had been. I couldn't understand how that was possible. Once more, I had the feeling that the line between my dreams and my waking reality were becoming obscured. At the Mother tree I gathered my belongings and, as we set off for the Centre, I was secure in the knowledge that I had lost sight of my sanity!

That evening as I was preparing for bed I heard the familiar sounds of coyotes at play. I got up from my hut and looked off towards the sound of the din. The desert was lit by the moon and I could see plainly. Across a clearing the powerful Alfa male emerged and we stood briefly staring at one another before he turned and disappeared into the night.

I stood there for a long time listening to the pack of mischievous killers and thieves move off merrily on their never-ending search. I wondered if I might be able to find them in my dreams. I wondered if I was dreaming at that moment. Daniel's teachings and this magical setting had my head spinning. My perception of reality had been upended and I no longer knew which way was up! At this point, I knew that I should be in a panic, but I was strangely at peace. I felt like I had spent my whole life in a blind, brainwashed coma and that I was now but a babe in a fascinating new world! When I crawled into my sleeping bag I was eager to see where I would go and what I could learn.

~•~

We were coming to the end of our stay at The Centre of the Conscious Dream and I, for one, was not excited about the prospect of leaving this place of revelations. Thanks to the awesome food prepared for us by the women in the village I had regained much of my strength during my stay. I was hoping that the food, the healing powers of the Mountain and desert, and the healing teachings from Daniel had vanquished my health issues.

Daniel told us that we had only three days left, and we needed to make some decisions. First, he asked us if we were interested in having a Peyote ceremony. I had come across the sacred plant of the Huichols several times in my explorations. They seemed to grow in colonies with a large mother cactus in the center of a cluster of her smaller offspring.

Of the four of us, Angelina and myself were the most enthusiastic, Tess and Marco seemed indifferent. They were excited about having a fire ceremony though and tomorrow night would be a full moon! Daniel said he would go into the desert and harvest enough of the sacred plant for the ceremony in the traditional way. I was not sure what all that involved, but was sure he would do it more respectfully than the goat herder would have.

The other decision we had to make was whether we would rather go to a small town in the mountains where we could do some shopping or have a ceremony on the mountainside. I was relieved when we were all of the same mind on this one. The Mountain was beckoning to all of us. The Mountain had been playing a large part in my dreams. She seemed omnipresent in them and there was always the suggestion of a crystal. This might be my chance to find a souvenir of my stay and of the Mountain herself.

~•~

The next day was a free day for us. Daniel was going into the desert and we could use it as a time to reflect and prepare for the night's ceremony. I chose the time to make some necklaces for my friends as that is a hobby of mine and I wanted to thank them for being such great companions in this adventure. I hoped that, by giving them something that I had made, we would always have a connection. It still amazes me that four strangers from different parts of the planet could come together and have such a powerful experience as we had.

Angelina had such a vibrant spirit! She had been called here by the Mountain to find her power. She lit up every conversation and soaked up the magic of the desert like a sponge. The bond we formed by burying each other had grown stronger and we will always have a special connection. To this day, we can, and often do, lean on each other.

Tess was simply a force of nature. She might have been older than me but her body and soul defied age. She was more fit than the other three of us put together! Her presence was ethereal and this was not her first spiritual journey. If the saying that the eyes are the window to the soul is true, then Tess's soul must be as vast as the universe. They were fathomless and emanated the peacefulness that only someone who is content with themselves and their world can show. She was a formidable dreamer and, most likely, a pillar of feminine power in her homeland.

Marco had been shy and unassuming and kept to himself a lot at first. As he warmed to us he seemed to come out of his shell and it was a wonderful thing to watch. Occasionally, he would floor us with a bit of his dry English wit. I would always fondly remember our morning spot of tea with Tess and Marco and the conversations that people from opposite sides of the earth would have.

That night Daniel showed us how to construct a fire for a fire/Peyote ceremony. He showed us how to open to the spirits of the Elements - Air, Fire, Earth and Water. He also opened to the spirits of Mother Earth and those of the Stars. Soon after opening the ceremony to the spirits, Daniel passed around a plate with chunks of the sacred plant. This plate made several more rounds, but my stomach told me when I had enough. I have no idea how the ceremony would have gone if I had partaken more of the sacred plant, but this evening I was listening to my body and it was telling me to be moderate. Nevertheless, the power of Daniel's song combined with the Mountain's energy and the altered perception of the sacred plant made the ceremony full of magic. We drummed and danced and, thankfully, Daniel didn't make me sing this time. Several times during the ceremony I could hear my coyote friends calling to Chapo and myself. Chapo was eager to go to them and I had to convince him otherwise.

The highlight of the enchanting ceremony was when the Mountain seemed to give birth to the full moon. We watched as the great moon rose from the mountaintop and fill the desert with a silvery light that inspired awe. With the rising of the moon Daniel ended the ceremony and left us to ride out our journey with the sacred plant of the desert. I found the effects of the Peyote to be very similar to that of its cousin, San Pedro. It cast a beautiful light on everything and brought you to be close to Mother Nature. It was not hallucinogenic in the amount I had eaten but was more of a heightening of the senses. Everything was more vivid and clear and mysterious in the half light.

Marco and Tess came out of their shells and laughed and sang. They told hilarious stories, cavorted and showed a youthful zest that belied their years. It was an extraordinary and bewitching adventure that served to cement the bond we felt. They were still going strong long after I had retired to my hut.

When I woke up the next morning there was a slight mist to the air and the compound was still in quiet slumber. There was a meditation spiral in the clearing beyond the temple hut and I walked it in what had become my morning ritual. When I got to the center I sat and opened to the sounds and smells of the stirring desert. We were going to the Mountain today and I was excited but sad that my time here was coming to an end. Chapo and I watched the sunrise and basked in the energy of the rising sun. The others wouldn't wake up for a while and I used the time to soak in as much of the spirit of this magical place as I could.

I considered the Mountain. During our work with conscious dreaming she had always been looming in the background with a message of a crystal. She seemed to me to be a living, conscious, immensely powerful creature that was lighting up this desert and speaking with the cosmos. She kept secrets that we mortals could not understand. We were going to the Mountain today to conduct a ceremony celebrating what we had learned and to honor the perfection of the Mountain, the perfection of ourselves and of the moment. I was celebrating the fact that she had summoned me here from Arizona. What she had created here was an environment where people could come and connect to cosmic energies that can guide them and help them in their everyday lives. I can't express the honor that I felt that she had reached out to me and deemed me worthy of her lessons. Today we would be five pilgrims setting out to pay homage and respect to this deity of the desert.

As I waited for the others I considered all that I had learned from Daniel. It was he who had invited me to the desert, but it was the Mountain who had called me. Daniel was a bit of an enigma to me. While he was sincere in his efforts to help us achieve what we had been called to the desert to learn, he always has an amused glint in his eye. He seemed to take delight in the uniqueness of each person's journey and showed a peaceful enthusiasm for their quest. He showed us the path and then marveled in the different routes we took to get there. He had taught me how to look at the world with a completely different perspective. The gift he had given me of accessing my dreams was life changing. I was just beginning to understand how powerful a tool it was to shape your reality. The ability to control your dreams was the ability to control your destiny!

In our meeting under the tree Daniel told us that we would be spending the day on the Mountain so we should pack a lunch and enough water. It was getting towards the end of November but the desert days were still hot. We piled into a pickup of one of Daniel's local buddies and set out for the Mountain. Our bumpy ride ended at the only store in a sleepy, almost deserted little village at the base of the mountain. At the trailhead just outside the village Daniel pulled out some Peyote left over from the fire ceremony the previous night and asked if any of us would like to partake in the last bits of his harvest. Angelina and I were the only ones to accept his offer. There were only a few chunks left and I chose to suck on the pieces given to me instead of chewing them up. By doing this, the effect was more gradual and easier on my stomach.

Daniel pointed to a natural terrace partway up the mountain and told us to follow Tess as it was not her first visit to the Mountain and that he would meet us there. Tess in turn set out at an impossible pace for someone of her years.

As we struggled to keep pace with the sprinting Tess, I was attracted to a small canyon that we passed on our climb to the meeting place. I instinctively started to walk towards it and was interrupted by a call from Angelina saying that Tess was taking another path. By this time Tess was leaving me in the dust and I had to hurry to catch up. I made a promise to myself to return if given the chance as it had unmistakably called to me and I usually liked to follow my instincts.

Daniel was waiting for us at the spot he had picked to make an offering to the Mountain. This was amazing to me as he had left after us and I had not seen him on the trail. He was busy laying out a medicine wheel with crystals that Tess had brought from Scotland. I sat at the spot he indicated and we were each given a crystal to make our offering to the magic Mountain.

Daniel told us to reflect on all that we had learned in the desert and to try to bring it all together in this breathtaking spot overlooking the desert below. We were here to seek the perfection of the Mountain. The perfection of our spirits and of the moment. We each buried our crystals and anointed them with water and stated our intentions to the cosmos. Daniel then started to play the flute as only he can and I was immediately transported. I have no idea how long he played, but it took me on a journey that revisited my time in the desert and all the magic that I had experienced here. My lessons were relearned and became part of who I am.

It is beyond me to describe my feelings as his song trailed off. The peyote, his song, the pristine setting and the beautiful vibrations being put forth from my comrades, all culminated in the most incredible lightness of being. I was at one with myself and my surroundings and my fellow seekers in a way that I have never thought possible! In that instant. In that perfect moment, I believe I found my place in the universe. It all made sense! All the teachings! All my trials and tribulations! All my missteps and victories! They all came together to make me who I am and to bring me to this incredible place with these amazing people! For the first time in my life I was aware of my power. Maybe for the first time in my life I was not afraid! And maybe, for the first time, I felt content with myself and my life. I felt with certainty that I was where I was supposed to be and my journey was on the right path!

With our ceremony completed Daniel told us to take the rest of the day and explore the Mountain and to try to learn why she had called us here in the first place. We all went our separate ways with the instruction to meet at the pickup in the village at sunset. Here was my chance to find my crystal that I believed I had been promised!

~•~

I started picking my way down the mountain. I was being called to the small canyon that I had reluctantly passed at the bottom. When I reached the canyon I stopped and ate lunch in the shade of a dry-stacked wall of an ancient horse or sheep pen. I wondered at who had built it and what kind of life they led.

When I was rested and had picked the various cactus needles from my legs, I started to explore the ravine. I had spied some caves on my way down the mountainside and was eager to check them out. It wasn't long before I came around a bend in the path to see Daniel sitting relaxed under a shade tree. How had he got there before me? I was getting a little disconcerted about how he seemed to be able jump in front of me without my being aware! He had that glint in his eye as he asked me where I was headed and I told him I had seen some caves on my way down. Daniel said that is where he was headed also, but that he had been there before and that I should go ahead by myself. I left him there looking slightly amused and continued my hike.

Walking up the wash I was constantly reminded of the beauty that surrounded me. The cactus and rocks, the birds and insects, they were all weaving a perfect complex web of existence. I was amazed at the diversity of life in a seemingly dry and hostile environment. Then I realized that it might be hostile, but it was beautiful in its severity. The creatures and plants that thrived here had found a way to survive in this arid land. That they could thrive here was a miracle to me and it made them all the more beautiful in my eyes. And, although this place was beautiful, my dwindling water bottle told me that it was not a place for the faint of heart.

As I hiked up the canyon the air shimmered under the blazing sun giving the illusion that I was looking through a thin veil of water. It was afternoon now and the sun was relentless! I spit out the piece of peyote that I had been sucking on and took a long draught of water to cleanse my palate of its distinctive taste. The canyon had an otherworldly feel to me. The sand and rocks seemed to be alive and gently vibrating in a complex harmony. If I listened closely I could almost hear them whispering to me. I was light-headed and beginning to see glimpses of things I wasn't sure about by the time I reached the first cave. I collapsed into the shade of its mouth and lay in the dirt of the floor of the cave relishing its coolness.

After a time, I began to recover from my peyote infused heat exhaustion and began to investigate. The floor of the cave was loose and sloped at an almost impossible angle. I scratched and clawed up the slope seemingly sliding back two feet for every one gained. I was tired and dirty and about to give up when the slope leveled off to a little ledge and the cave came to an abrupt end.

There was no light here. I could hear squeaks and feel whispers of air and whiffs of ammonia and I realized I had squirmed into the cave's belfry of bats! I was surprised by the fact that I was not afraid of my furry hosts. On the contrary, I felt strangely at ease in the cool depths and

I relaxed completely and closed my eyes. My last thought was of my task to find the perfection of the Mountain and of my quest for a crystal.

No sooner than I had closed my eyes, I was swept up in a dream. All Daniel's teachings over the last few weeks of conscious dreaming, dreaming with intent, were paying off! I had a strange feeling of melting into the rock surface of the cave. My body was absorbed by the Mountain herself and I felt myself falling into her depths. I was mesmerized by the site of many wondrous things that I had no idea could exist inside a mountain! There were streams and waterfalls! There were blind fish and long-legged spiders! I saw incredible crystal caverns and veins of pure silver and gold!

The Mountain was an ancient creature. She was here before all others. She has seen oceans come and go. She held the wisdom of the Earth and kept untold secrets. Her knowledge was vast and her power was immense! Her memories were of creation itself!

She showed me many things that I never could have imagined and then she showed me something that I would never forget.

She was home to a hugely diverse ecosystem and her maternal instincts were to nurture and protect her children. One of her children had become ill, however. In their fever, these men had burrowed like parasites and riddled the mountain in the sickness of their greed for gold and silver.

My intuition that she was a creature of wisdom was confirmed when she opened her heart to me. Despite being one of the parasitical beings that was consuming her like a cancer, she had the dignity to grant my wish. Maybe our ceremony had proven to her that we had only respect. I descended into what could only be the heart of this magical Mountain. I found myself in a cavern of crystals that stunned and bedazzled me! The rainbow of hues from the infinite facets of the crystals was hypnotic. In the center of the cavern was the source of the light that made the crystals shimmer. A huge red crystal glowed softly and seemed to pulse a steady, slow rhythm. I had no doubt that this omnipotent Mountain was revealing her very heart to me!

This was the source of the crystal that had been promised and it was far more than any I could have imagined! I was humbled to the core of my being as I considered the blessing that had been bestowed upon me. I had seen things that I wasn't sure I had the right to see. She was indeed an ancient living entity that had been there at the beginning and would be there at the end. Our lives were but a fleeting whisper to her song. I was amazed at the destruction that we, insignificant as we are, were capable of in our masses.

In an instant, I was back in the cave and moving like I was being helped to exit. I realized that I was sliding down the slope of the cave towards the light at the bottom. I had the eerie feeling that I was being given birth through the Mountain's womb. When I hit bottom of the slope I sprawled out into the sunlight. A feeling of renewal washed over me and I felt like my energy had been replenished. I felt like I had been symbolically reborn! The fulfilled promise of a crystal was beyond my imaginings and the insights of the Mountain's character were forever imprinted in my soul.

I had no idea how long I had been in the cave. The shadows were getting long and the worst of the heat had passed so I decided to start back towards the village while there was still some light. The Mountain, it seemed, was hesitant to let me go as the trail back looked nothing like the one we had come in on. I trusted my sense of direction and after a few wrong turns I found my way back to the village and the corner store. None of my friends were around so I bought a bottle of water and climbed in the pickup to wait.

The store was the gathering place for the villagers and as the sun's light faded they started to show up and hang out. They couldn't help but be curious about the stranger in the back of the truck. They were a friendly bunch and it appeared that they didn't have much contact with gringos as they were full of questions. I explained that I was waiting for four others that hadn't yet returned from the Mountain. We all got more concerned as the light faded. Before the light was completely gone I walked back to the edge of town and was relieved to see Daniel and Marco emerge out of the twilight. When I told him that Angelina and Tess weren't back yet he told me to go back to the store and wait there while he and Marco started back up the trail to find them. Although I wanted to help in the search Daniel wanted me at the store in case they came in by another route.

While I was getting worried and wanted to look for my friends Daniel was unfazed as always. He said that this had happened before and not to worry. When I got back to the store it seemed the whole village had turned out. I guess the word had gotten out that there were some lost gringos wandering around in the dark. They were either more concerned about the situation than Daniel was or maybe it was a bit of excitement in a usually quiet town.

Again, I was amazed at their kindness and the concern they showed for total strangers. Although they had very little themselves they offered me food and drink and would take no payment in return. You would not know it by their actions, but this was one of the poorest regions in the country, and these people really struggled to survive in this harsh environment. Employment was few and far between as the mines were struggling and facing opposition from the indigenous people of the area. Opportunities were nearly nonexistent for these people. I was amazed that these people who faced such hardship would wait and worry with me.

They were very curious about what had brought me to the Mountain. I tried to explain to them that they lived in a magical place and that I had come here to learn and grow as a person. As always, they wanted to know of the United States. I did my best to convince them that it is not what it is cracked up to be and that, if given the choice of where to live, I would choose this majestic desert. They were lured by the promise of opportunity I was lured by the simplicity of their existence.

Their concern was growing as darkness fell and I could hear them begin to plan a rescue if my friends didn't return soon. Although they wouldn't take any money, I found a way to repay them for their kindness with a donation toward a big fiesta they were planning soon. They would only accept my offer if I promised to return and celebrate with them.

The last time I had seen Tess she was heading up to the top of the Mountain. That she had the fortitude to attempt to summit the Mountain did not surprise me. I had long since stopped being amazed by her. As impressive as Tess was, she had become disoriented on her return much as I had. She was the first to show up and she waited with Marco at the trailhead for Daniel and Angelina.

I understand that Daniel found Angelina by her singing. She had attempted to follow Tess up the mountain and hadn't been able to keep up with Tess's unflagging spirit and pace. When she had turned back she came down the wrong ridge and had become disoriented. As the light faded, so did her hopes of finding the elusive trail back to town. She must have been terrified at the prospect of spending the night alone on the Mountain. Even in her growing terror she had the intuition to start singing and that is what led Daniel to her. I think the Mountain had been attracted to Angelina's inner light and had disoriented her in its reluctance to let her go.

Several of the villagers had already headed out to start rounding up horses for a search when my companions finally made it to the store. As we drove back down to the Centre I couldn't help but be impressed with the honor and graciousness of the people of the village.

~•~

I had found my promised crystal and though I could not hold it in my hand, it is indelibly etched in my mind and heart. Our time in the desert had come to an end and I was reluctant. In some way I felt that I was protected here. Daniel and the desert had gifted me some tools and life lessons that would prove to be invaluable to me in the near future. The magical Mountain had called to me in the nick of time and I would be in need of everything I had learned shortly. Daniel's most important gift to me, the art of conscious dreaming, had changed my whole way of looking at the world and the universe. The Mother Ayahuasca had opened my eyes to all the infinite possibilities that I had been blind to and Daniel's teachings had given me real tools with which I was able to access some of them. I felt like I had just scratched the surface of some of the mysteries of the cosmos and of our lives as we know it. The mere fact that we manifest our own reality was mind shattering and changed my whole approach to this journey we call life.

Today was our last day and the hardest for me. I would miss Daniel, my new friends, the Mountain, my Mother tree, and my trickster animal guides. It was hard to say farewell, but I knew in my heart that this was not goodbye. This place and these remarkable people were an integral part of me now and I knew that they would always be a part of my dream.

As a parting gift Daniel did a reading on me. He used tarot cards but his main method was to simply have me lay down as he cradled my head in his hands and invoked the entities that were his guides. I was planning on continuing my studies into the mysteries of life that I had just begun to scratch the surface of and I asked Daniel what he thought about that.

After consulting with his teachers, his answer to me was surprising. He said that I was full of inner turmoil. There was a battle being waged inside me and that my first priority was to resolve it. He said that if I could find my inner peace then the universe would be at my fingertips. At the time, I thought he was referring to my conflicting emotions about leaving my family and friends behind and going on this journey. I would soon find out what kind of inner battle he was referring to and it was not to be what I expected.

Chapter Seven
Inner Turmoil

After saying our heartfelt farewells Chapo and I loaded up and headed south with no clear destination in mind. As soon as we left the sanctuary of the magical Mountain things took a sharp turn for the worse for me. My stomach malady returned in full force and within a couple days I was struggling, once again, to find the nourishment that I needed. Three weeks later I would wake up on the floor of the shower of my room in Playa de Carmen with Chapo licking my face. When I went to a local doctor he took one look at my blood work and told me I should catch the next flight back to the United States. Not tomorrow, the next flight today. The look on his face left no doubt in my mind that I did not have any choice in the matter.

When Chapo and I got to the airport in Cancun I simply walked up to the ticket counter and said that I needed help. The clerk took one look at me and called the manager. I explained my situation to him and he took over. He helped me park my truck in a safe long-term parking lot and got me on the first flight to the States.

I convinced them that Chapo was a service dog and he acted the part admirably.

I was weak and delirious and remember little of the flight home. Chapo was amazing and I think he knew something was wrong because he stayed close and attentive. The airline staff was incredible. They met me at the gate in Fort Worth with a wheel chair and got me through customs and on my connecting flight to Tucson.

When I got there my nephew met me and took custody of Chapo and got me to the hospital. The doctors at the hospital immediately put me on a high regimen of antibiotics and a lethal dose of pain killers. I was already delirious and the high dose of dilaudid sent me into never-never land. The next couple of days were a blur to me. When not sleeping I might as well have been because I had no idea what was going on. I was aware that they were performing a barrage of tests on me in between my rather bizarre dreams.

A couple of days after my admission, my drug induced euphoria was shattered when a doctor came in and told me I had a cholangiocarcinoma tumor in my liver and that my chances of survival were not good. He said that I would probably not be leaving the hospital and should start putting my affairs in order.

The news sent me reeling. At this point, I had no idea if I had dreamt the episode or not. One thing I knew was that I was in no condition to make any decisions and I immediately asked to be taken off the mind-bending pain meds. I had one more night of barely knowing where I was, or who was who.

The next day my head began to clear and the gravity of my situation started to dawn on me. To say I was devastated would be to put it mildly. My first thought was of Chapo. How could I abandon my dog? I had told him that I would never leave him again. When I began to make the phone calls and tell my family what was happening I was assured that Chapo was in good hands no matter what happened. The knowledge that Chapo would be taken care of freed me to consider my situation. I have to admit; when I first heard the news I was terrified. I still wasn't convinced that I hadn't dreamt the doctor's announcement.

My worst fears were confirmed when I was visited by a panel of doctors that barely fit in my room. There was a gastroenterologist, an oncologist, a surgeon and several others. They told me that based on the MRI results the radiologists were convinced that, by the quick onslaught of my illness and the size and appearance of the tumor, it was a fatal form of cancer that was manifesting as a tumor in my liver. They said it had tendrils that were strangling the portal vein in my liver and that it was well advanced. They were going to attempt a biopsy but that it was in a very tricky place and that the biopsy might be dangerous.

As I digested all this information, they informed me that, if they could not determine the nature of the tumor, then they could not treat it with chemo. They strongly recommended that I have an operation to cut the tumor out. This was a huge operation called a "whipple." The operation would involve removing some or all of my liver and the remaining half of my pancreas. They would then have to rearrange things to make it work at a basic level.

This was all very overwhelming for me, to say the least. I told them there was no way they were going to operate without knowing for sure what kind of tumor it was. They scheduled the biopsy and I had a day or two before the procedure to consider my options.

After the initial shock and subsequent terror that ensued I began to realize that I was not really afraid to die. What really scared me was the quality of life I would have after the operation. At this point I had been in and out of the hospital for the last five years. My chronic episodes of pancreatitis had made sure that, for much of this time, I had been in severe pain. With the exception of the break of a year or so when I was able to go to Peru and Mexico, my life had been pretty miserable. I had a good idea of what my quality of life would be after the operation they proposed and it did not appeal to me. I had met several people who had the operation and their life was not one that I wanted to experience. The operation might extend my life, but the quality of that life was not the way I wanted to live out my remaining days. The doctors spent some time attempting to convince me that some people lived for years after the operation and had fairly normal lives. The doctors were not happy with my decision to say the least.

The biopsy was scheduled and I had a couple of days to sit back and reflect on my predicament. My initial terror had faded with the haze of the pain meds and the lessons that I had learned started to emerge. I came to the realization that I was not afraid of death. During the last five years I had faced my share of pain and the prospect of a respite had some appeal to me.

The problem with that was the fact that I was not ready to die. I had some outstanding promises that I intended to keep. The first was to my dog Chapo. I told him I would never leave him again and I had already been separated from him for a week now. I imagined that he thought I had abandoned him again and it was breaking my heart.

The second promise had been made to Tatyana and the Mother Ayahuasca. I had promised to tell my story and spread the word about plant healing and that is what I intended to do.

My new perspective on life about it being a dream was exerting itself. In my retrospection, I came to the conclusion that, in the first part of the dream of my life I had abused alcohol and spent most of my time depressed. It turned out that my body wasn't as equipped for alcohol abuse as some people and I had paid a dire price for it. I was not a happy person although I tried to put on a happy face. I never had a clear vision of where my life was headed and often felt like I was a victim; that life owed me something and I was not getting it. Mother Ayahuasca had forced me to see the truth of my addictions and I was now realizing that I had made myself sick. I had chosen to go down that road and now I was paying the price. It also became clear to me that what you put into your body, mentally and physically, is what ultimately determines what you are made of. If you put enough toxins and negative thoughts into it then you will end up poisoning yourself. I had the feeling that maybe I was finally starting to grow up.

On the heels of these insights came another thought. My life was a dream and I had dreamed myself into a rather difficult situation. If that was the case, then shouldn't it be possible that I could dream myself out of this mess? Mother Ayahuasca had shown me that nothing was impossible!

I am fortunate to have a dear friend named Mia who was an amazing doctor and who has changed paths and gone into holistic medicine. She is an incredible healer with remarkable diagnostic instincts. She has helped many people who could not afford traditional treatments or had been shut out by the medical community.

When she came to visit me she had an in-depth talk with the gastroenterologist. She could actually speak their language and saw my condition in a clearer way than I ever could. She told me that, while the radiologists insisted that this was a cancerous tumor, the doctor she spoke with said that it was not like anything he had seen before. While it had characteristics of a cholangiocarcinoma tumor with tendrils radiating out, it also showed signs that it could be some kind of exotic infection. She is an empath and an angel, and I respected her opinion above anyone else's. I asked her if the tumor was some kind of unknown infection then wouldn't it be possible to heal from an infection. She told me that it was absolutely possible.

That was all I needed to hear.

The next day they took me down to do the needle biopsy. I was uneasy about this because they would have to go through my liver to get a good sample. This was not without inherent dangers. They prepped me and wheeled me into the operating room where I lay on the table for about an hour waiting for the doctor. In the meantime the nurses tried to keep me distracted by small talk about their children and lives. We avoided talking about mine. As the time passed I was growing more and more uneasy. Finally, the doctor came into the room and said he was sorry and that he couldn't, in good conscience, do the procedure as it was just too dangerous. Believe it or not this was a huge relief to me as I had been just about to call it off myself.

The next day the team of doctors was back in my room. My head was a lot clearer this time around and I felt like I was in better condition to make the biggest decision in my life. Since they weren't able to do the biopsy, chemotherapy was not an option, as they did not know what kind of tumor they were dealing with. This was fine with me as I did not believe in chemotherapy.

They then went on to tell me that the only other option and my only hope was the afore-mentioned surgery. When I declined their offer to cut it out they all stood around looking like I hadn't understood. I thought that I better explain myself. I told them that I had one major surgery already that had turned out not to be necessary and I was not about to have another! It was about quality of life for me. I was not about to torture myself to buy five more years of hell. The doctors argued that they had made improvements in the surgery and that one of their patients had lasted seven years. I said that I bet it was not a fun seven years and again declined their offer.

The frustration on the doctors' faces was evident as they explained that, without surgery, I would not survive. When I told them that I would rather die out in the sunshine then have 5-7 years of misery they left shaking their heads.

When I told Mia what the doctors had said she agreed with them. She said that she had also heard that they had made improvements and that I should consider the operation. I knew she only wanted what was best for me and for my pain to end. She couldn't know how I felt about another major surgery, how tired I was, or how important that quality of life was to me. She just wanted her friend's suffering to end. When I told her that I had made up my mind, I could see something change in her eyes. She had the look of someone who was saying goodbye to a friend; a tinge of sadness had crept in. It was suddenly evident to me that she didn't think this was something that I could overcome. I would have to get used to that look as I could see it in my family's eyes also. As I got skinnier pretty much everyone that looked at me thought that I had escaped from a POW camp. The worst part was when little children looked afraid when I smiled at them.

The doctors kept me there two more days to finish the antibiotic regimen that they were giving me. The contingent of doctors would make one more attempt to talk some sense into me and I respectfully declined once again. This time they showed their displeasure with me and made me sign a paper saying I was declining their recommended treatment. When I asked the gastro doctor how much time he thought I might have he said, rather testily, that he had no idea, but probably no more than a month. He told me that if I was still around in a month they would like to do another MRI and see what was happening.

After an endless amount of paperwork I made my escape and my brother picked me up and took me to his home where Chapo was waiting. If dogs can have surprised faces, then that is how Chapo looked when he saw me. It was obvious that he had given up on me again, but this time instead of being mad he was happier then I had ever seen him. My heart soared!

Chapter 8
Transcendence

After I left the hospital I still wasn't able to eat. My friend Mia went to the store with me and she helped me pick out the very basics; things that she thought I might have success keeping down. For the first two weeks the only things I managed to keep down was broth and clear soups. I was staying alive, but I was not going to get better like that. I needed sustenance, as my Mother Tree would have told me.

My friend Steve, who is a local farmer specializing in cannabis, had told me once that he had made a concentrated form of the sacred plant that had healed his friend of cancer. Having read a lot about Marijuana healing many different things, I decided to approach him about making some for me. I knew from past experience that the healing plant would make you have the munchies, if it could also help me with my tumor; I thought it would be worth a try. What did I have to lose?

When I asked Steve about it he said he knew how to make something he called "phoenix tears" and he would be willing to make a batch for me. I told him my funds were running low and he accepted what I could pay him, but he did it mostly out of the kindness of his heart. The money I paid him probably didn't come close to covering his costs.

The first time I took a dose it put me on the ground. There was no way I could function as even a semi-normal person. I was having a hard time sleeping because of pain so I decided to take the medicine right before attempting to go to sleep. It knocked me out cold for ten hours! The next day I found it much easier to keep food down.

Soon I was graduating to stewed vegetables. Looking back on it, I believe the "phoenix tears" were exactly what my body needed. They allowed me to get good deep sleep and my diet kept progressing. If this miracle plant could also work on my tumor then I might have a fighting chance. The only thing that bothered me is that I had no dreams! My dreams had become my life. This would be a difficult time for me as I had come to rely on my dreams to guide me.

Steve ended up making me three months' worth of his secret potion and in that time I steadily improved. To this day I take CBD oil every day. I really believe in the capacity that Marijuana has for healing. CBD has no THC in it so there are no side effects.

I will not lie. My pain was excruciating and the loss of my dreams often left me stuck in a place that resembled a nightmare. Several times I thought seriously about giving up. It was in those times when I felt little hope that Chapo would come and stare into my eyes like he was trying to tell me something. In his eyes I would see all the things we had been through and sometimes I could see a little of what might be still to come. He was not giving up on me and in return I would not give up on him.

The first month, (which felt much longer), passed and I went in for my MRI as I had been told to do. The oncologist could not treat me, but he was the doctor who was going to monitor my illness and interpret the MRIs for me. The tumor had not changed in size and he told me that was very encouraging. He said that he had thought it would have spread by now. I did not tell him about the "phoenix tears" and he did not ask. He told me to come back for another scan in a month.

The second scan showed that the tumor had actually shrunk a tiny bit. His mouth was open, and he was scratching his head. He was amazed that I had actually gained back a couple of pounds. He told me to come back in three months for another scan. That is of course unless I was forced to come back sooner.

My next scan showed that the tumor had shrunk a little more. My doctor was VERY happy. I had gained a couple more pounds and he was excited for me. He told me to keep doing whatever I was doing and to come back in three more months. By this time I was eating cooked veggies which were much easier on my palate.

My supply of "phoenix tears" was gone by now, but I know that without Steve's gift I would not have made it through those first months. I did not want to take advantage of Steve's generosity so I did not bother him for more. I was starting to believe again, and my dreams were coming back, which helped me have hope.

My sister was going through a very difficult time herself. She had come down with a rare immune system disease and was going to a doctor in Hermosillo, Mexico for treatment. It was a four-hour drive south of Bisbee. She was seeing an incredible holistic doctor. His name was Dr. Jesus Gonzalo Navarro Sota and he had a gentle manner about himself that exuded a strong sense of empathy. I think a lot of his treatment was based on intuition.

Dr. Gonzalo, as we referred to him, specialized in the use of a machine called a Mora. This incredible machine used biofeedback to analyze your body's electromagnetic frequencies. It could detect areas that were not emitting healthy frequencies and then fix them by emitting the opposite frequencies into those areas. I do not claim to understand it fully, but I asked my sister if I could go with her on her next trip. We ended up staying three weeks and going daily to the clinic. He also did intravenous ozone and vitamin C infusions. We had to come home after three weeks due to running low on money, but, when I left, I felt as if I had turned a corner.

When I returned to the states my next scan showed more improvement. My doctor was amazed again. He said that cancer never shrinks so it could not be cancer; it had to be something else. He sent me to the CDC to see if they could identify some kind of infection. After many tests, they said they could not diagnose the tumor either.

The doctors got together again and started to try and figure out different tests that could identify my illness and none were successful. At this point, I was dreaming again and, in one special dream, I went inside myself and saw the culprit firsthand. It was an ugly, nasty looking entity. I tried to get a feel for my adversary. I talked to my tumor. I told it that I was no longer mistreating my body and I no longer needed it to show me the error of my ways. I told it that I had changed, that my dream had changed and that there was really no place for the tumor in my new dream. My tumor did not speak back to me, but I felt like we had a better understanding of each other.

I had been so impressed with the Dr. Gonzalo in Mexico and his Mora machine that I sought out a slightly eccentric genius inventor that just happened to live in Bisbee. He had invented a machine based on the same principles as the Mora machine.

In the 1930's a doctor named Royal Rife invented an optical microscope with which he could see microbes that could not previously be seen. He also discovered that diseases emitted certain electromagnetic frequencies. He found that they could be destroyed by bombarding them with different frequencies. He claimed he could destroy cancer in this manner and could actually see it happen with his optical microscope. He was discredited and censured by the AMA who had no interest in a cure for cancer.

My new friend, Byington, had invented a machine he called a "galvanic bath" that worked on the same principals. His machine emitted electric pulses at the same frequencies established by Dr. Rife. I met Byington at his house for a demonstration of his machine. The disturbing part of his treatment was that it used water to conduct the frequencies. This meant you had to immerse yourself in water and hold a handheld device that emitted electronic frequencies at your problem area. This was disconcerting to say the least. The device pulsed 30 amps at rapid speeds. At first, I was reluctant to sit in water with any amount of electricity involved. Byington demonstrated the device by sitting in a hot tub. Sure enough, it didn't kill him.

With some trepidation, I sat in the tub and turned on the machine. It seemed to pull at places where I knew I had problems such as my shoulders where I had arthritis and my lower back where I had a pinched nerve resulting in sciatic nerve pain. When I directed it at my liver it went ballistic and I could feel it causing spasms. It seemed that if you held it to a problem area the spasms it created would lessen until they faded away. The spasms in my liver did not fade away and I knew that I wouldn't be cured in one sitting. My shoulders and lower back, however; felt instantly better after the treatment. He showed me an app that I could download to my phone that had a list of the frequencies to destroy almost any malady you could think of. I was so impressed that I bought one of his machines with my dwindling monetary resources. I found a used hot tub that someone just wanted hauled off and commenced to treat myself. I set my machine to emit frequencies to kill Candida carcinomas and started to use it three times a week. After a few weeks of use, the spasms it caused in my liver began to lessen. I took this as a good sign. I was feeling no worse for the treatment so I hoped that it was having a positive effect and was not causing me any harm.

After my next MRI the oncologist was very excited to see me. He told me that the scan showed marked improvement! He was animated, and he asked me just how I was treating myself. I asked him why he was suddenly interested. He replied that up until then they had considered me as terminal. When I told him about the galvanic bath the doctor went pale and just stared at me for a moment. He then excused himself, saying he would be right back. He returned with two other doctors in tow. He asked me to repeat what I had told him. When I was done, the doctors looked at me like I was insane and they all three went back out the door.

When he returned the oncologist said that they could not condone sitting in a hot tub with electrical currents running through it. He told me that there was no way that the galvanic bath could have any effect on my tumor. I asked him if the machine wasn't working then how come I was getting better. His reply was that I believed that it was working and that my belief was making me better. I was not going to argue the point with him. I could not prove that the machine was the cause for my recovery. And I did not mention to him that I was dreaming my tumor away. He would have had me locked up. He was already looking at me strangely and I thought it better not to push my luck. I still use my machine three times a week to this day.

By this time, I was convinced that I was going to be alright. My dream of traveling through Central and South America had been dashed as traveling all the time was just too hard on me. The good thing about dreams is they are flexible. I needed a new goal. I had a vision of working with the land, of feeling my hands in the soil. In my whole life I had never had the opportunity to have a garden. I dreamt that I could grow my own food. I decided to spend the rest of what little savings I had left on a little place in the desert outside Bisbee. It needed some work, but it had nine acres and a well. I had to be very careful how much I could do without setting myself back physically, which I did several times. It took all my self-control not to overdo it. When I started my move I could only do about an hour of physical activity before collapsing in exhaustion. My energy returned in baby steps and each day I was able to do just a little more. Then one day I realized that I was actually hungry! And guess what? As soon as my hunger returned I realized that I was also happy again.

All my teachings flooded back into my brain. As I realized that I was being given yet one more chance at life, my appreciation for just how beautiful life is also returned. I slowed down and looked around in wonder once again. The sky, the moon, the stars, my friends, all seemed new and more precious to me. I was excited to see what I could manifest in my new home out in the desert. Each day at sunset I would walk my meditation spiral and, when I reached the center, I would stop and try to connect with my surroundings. I would concentrate on my breathing and try to feel the vibration of the Earth through my feet. Once I felt in rhythm with my world I would start moving in the way Daniel had shown me. In my dance with Mother Nature I would try to release all the toxic things that had attached themselves to me during the day. As I danced I would sing to my tumor, hoping to ease it along its way out of my body. Gradually I began to appreciate each moment for what it was. Slowly

I remembered that each moment was all there was. The drive to get things done diminished as I saw that things would get done or they wouldn't. I had a whole dream ahead of me and in that dream the most important thing was to be happy.

After my last MRI my oncologist declared that my tumor was resolved. He said there was no need to come back. He also told me that he had never had the opportunity to release a patient without having ever treated them and it felt good. In my last conversation with my gastroenterologist I asked him what he thought my prognosis was. He asked me if I really sat in water and ran electricity through my body. When I told him that I did, he just laughed and shook his head. He said that when he first met me he thought I wouldn't last a month. When I reminded him that they had tried three times to convince me to have surgery he apologized and said that's the only thing they could think of to save my life. Before we parted he said to me, "Mister Taylor, I think you will live exactly as long as you want to."

My journey, which was set off by a little piece of calcium stuck in my pancreas, has been a remarkable one. It has taken me to the darkest depths of my soul. A lonely place where it is very bleak and hopeless. It has also taken me to incredible places I never knew existed. It has rekindled my sense of wonder at the beautiful complexity of nature and appreciation for this dream we call life. Although a good portion of my journey involved pain and uncertainty, I don't think I would change a thing. The trials and tribulations that I have been through forged me into who I am today. I have exorcised many of my demons that had been holding me back and can truly say that I am happy with who I am.

If you can take but two things from my tale; I hope they would be to never, ever give up and to not be afraid to dream!

Author's Notes:

I believe each of the formidable plant medicines discussed in this book; Ayahuasca, Peyote, San Pedro and Marijuana have powerful spirits and their own personalities. I cannot stress how important it is to have respect for these entities; they demand it. Abuse of these plants can be dangerous to your soul. They have a dark side to them that will make you pay for disrespect. That is why being guided in a ceremony by someone who is a trained shaman is the only way I would recommend asking them for help. Each of these sacred plants has different characteristics, but they are all potent physical and spiritual healers.

The ingredient in Ayahuasca that takes you on the psychedelic tour of the universe is called dimethyltryptamine or DMT. This molecule is found in hundreds of plants and even in the human body itself. It is widely believed that your body releases a large amount of DMT at the moment of death and that is what catapults the spirit into the afterlife. Ayahuasca is an amazing healer of psychological disorders. It is being researched for its ability to help heal everything from depression and addictions to every sort of mental trauma. The main side effect of this sacred plant is that it is sometimes difficult to re-integrate back into mainstream life as it shows you the world without illusions. Unfortunately, seeing things as they really are has its downfalls, as it will make you very aware of all the mistruths and injustices that are prevalent in our society. Ayahuasca is a stern teacher and her revelations can come at a price. The Mother Ayahuasca was by far the most potent of these healing plants. Her spirit can seem very dark as she will take you on a journey within. This can be tortuous and terrifying. She can also take you to places that are beyond beautiful. It seemed to me that she was going to purge me of my toxins and make me confront my demons before I was worthy of her more enlightening gifts. There is no doubt that Mother Ayahuasca will change your life. You had best go into it with the knowledge that you will be changed forever, because I don't think there is any way around it. The fact that the real shamans that are trained to work with the Mother plant are located in very remote and therefore somewhat dangerous locations is another factor. I was very fortunate to be with a group that honored the plant and her traditions in a peaceful setting. I cannot stress how perilous it could be to try and find a good shaman on your own. There are just too many things that can go wrong, and you are putting yourself in a very vulnerable position.

San Pedro, the father plant of the Peruvians is the lightest of the sacred plants and it will take you on a physical and mental odyssey that I found to be euphoric. I believe the father plant opened up my senses to things that they had gone blind to. It was a very spiritually enlightening experience for me. San Pedro is a gentler healer than Ayahuasca and more forgiving. His teaching methods are less severe. He showed me just how magnificent and exhilarating place this planet of ours is. I don't believe that it has the lasting and personality changing effects of Ayahuasca.

I am least familiar with Peyote, the sacred plant favored by the Huichol Indians of Mexico. It may be a little more potent than San Pedro. It is also very physical and maybe a little more hallucinogenic than its cousin. I could see Peyote's spirit being more demanding and vengeful and she seems like she would exact a high price for abuse. I remember the rather vacant look on the shepherd I had met in the desert. It seemed to me that the powerful plant was no longer helping him. It had taken his soul someplace where there is not a lot of light.

Marijuana is the least psychoactive in my opinion. She is also the most potent healer. We are just starting to realize the many benefits she can offer. Her best healing is done on a physical level, while the previous three work more on our subconscious, mental and spiritual levels. Marijuana may have unforetold medicinal benefits, but even she has a dark side. She can be a seductive mistress and before long, without your even being aware of it, she can make you crave for her release. While her dark side is not as dangerous as the others, I don't think there is any doubt that abusing her will dull your wits and affect your overall energy.

I am a huge believer in the healing property of all these sacred plants. I think we will never know all the benefits that they offer. I am also of the opinion that, as with all things, moderation is the best course. The beautiful and powerful spirits have the ability to steal your soul and take it to a place where they can enslave you. I think it takes a certain amount of strength to deal with these entities in a mature fashion and their teaching methods might be difficult for the faint of heart.

About the Author

Chris was born in 1957, the seventh of ten children. After working many years in construction and architecture, this is Chris' first attempt at writing a book. He has made a full recovery from a mysterious and life-threatening tumor with the help of healing plant medicines and the power of his dreams. Chris is currently living with his dog Chapo and trying to connect with Mother Nature in the Sonoran Desert outside of Bisbee, Arizona. He is continuing his work with his spirit guides on his quest to master the art of Conscious Dreaming and is contemplating his next adventure.

Printed by BoD™ in Norderstedt, Germany